Fictitious Capital

Fictitious Capital

How Finance is Appropriating Our Future

Cédric Durand

Translated by David Broder

VERSO
London • New York

For Jeanne, Loul and Isidore

The translation of this books was supported by the Centre national du livre (CNL).

Avec le soutien du

Cet ouvrage publié dans le cadre du programme d'aide à la publication bénéficie du soutien du Ministère des Affaires Etrangères et du Service Culturel de l'Ambassade de France représenté aux Etats-Unis. This work received support from the French Ministry of Foreign Affairs and the Cultural Services of the French Embassy in the United States through their publishing assistance program.

English-language edition first published by Verso 2017
Originally published in French as *Le capital fictif*
© Les Prairies ordinaires 2014
Translation © David Broder 2017

1 3 5 7 9 10 8 6 4 2

Verso
UK: 6 Meard Street, London W1F 0EG
US: 20 Jay Street, Suite 1010, Brooklyn, NY 11201
versobooks.com

Verso is the imprint of New Left Books

ISBN-13: 978-1-78478-719-6 (PB)
ISBN-13: 978-1-78663-284-5 (HB)
ISBN-13: 978-1-78478-720-2 (UK EBK)
ISBN-13: 978-1-78478-721-9 (US EBK)

British Library Cataloguing in Publication Data
A catalogue record for this book is available from the British Library

Library of Congress Cataloging-in-Publication Data

Names: Durand, Câedric, author.
Title: Fictitious capital : how finance is appropriating our future / Câedric
  Durand ; translated by David Broder.
Other titles: Capital fictif. English
Description: London ; Brooklyn, NY : Verso, 2017. | "Originally published in
  French as Le capital fictif : Les Prairies ordinaies, 2014." | Includes
  bibliographical references and index.
Identifiers: LCCN 2016058500 | ISBN 9781784787196 (alk. paper)
Subjects: LCSH: Finance. | Capitalism.
Classification: LCC HG173.3 .D8713 2017 | DDC 332–dc23
LC record available at https://lccn.loc.gov/2016058500

Typeset in Minion by MJ & N Gavan, Truro, Cornwall
Printed and bound by CPI Group (UK) Ltd, Croydon, CR0 4YY

Contents

List of Tables and Figures

Data and sources are available online at cedricdurand.eu

Acknowledgements

This book owes a lot to the unrelenting enthusiasm of Nicolas Vieilles-cazes and Razmig Keucheyan. All hail Nicolas for his patient editing work! I am also very grateful to David Broder for his meticulous translation and to Verso's editors. I would especially like to thank Sebastian Budgen for his sober but constant support.

I carried out my research at the Centre d'Économie de Paris Nord on the Villetaneuse campus of the Université Paris-13, a great place to work. This book would never have seen the light of day if it were not for the countless discussions I had with colleagues there and the helping hand they provided. Here I am particularly thinking of Emmanuel Carré, Benjamin Coriat, David Flacher, Ariane Ghirardello, Dany Lang, Marc Lautier, Antonia Lopez-Villavicencio, Jonathan Marie, Jacques Mazier, Pascal Petit, Dominique Plihon, Nathalie Rey, Sandra Rigot, Francisco Serranito and Julien Vauday. So, too, the dynamic team of doctoral students and young postdocs communing at our lunchtime political-economy seminar: Raquel Almeida Ramos, Félix Boggio, Louison Cahen Fourot, Bruno Carballa, Matteo Cavallaro and Léonard Moulin.

I should make special mention of the generous efforts of Robert Guttman, who took the time to read a first version of this work and discuss it with me in some depth. Tristan Auvray and Céline Baud were also kind enough to read over a draft of the first chapters and share their judicious suggestions. Grégoire Chamayou lent his attentive ear to the development of this book and shared his insights. Sebastian Budgen, Philippe Légé and Bruno Tinel each suggested valuable references. Critical comments by Julien Vercueil, Guillaume Fondu and Eve Chiapello, as well as John Grahl's report preceding this English translation, allowed me to refine the text and to clear up certain ambiguities.

My exchanges with Jerry Epstein, William Milberg, André Orléan, Riccardo Bellofiore and Éric Pineault helped feed my thinking. The arguments developed in the final chapter owe a great deal to my work together with Engelbert Stockhammer and Sébastien Miroudot. The book as a whole also reflects my lively collaboration with François Chesnais, Esther Jeffers, Stathis Kouvelakis and Michel Husson, who all did much to inspire it.

I would also like to thank *Les Anges* for having provided a perfect home for our editorial meetings, before they were cut down by fanatics' bullets on 13 November 2015.

The Sign of Autumn

One of the most remarkable developments in the rich countries since the 1970s has been the accelerated expansion of financial operations. The 2007–8 crisis and the long recession in which the world economy has been caught up ever since have brutally exposed the exorbitant economic and social cost of such financialisation. Yet nothing suggests that our societies are on a path to freeing themselves from its grip. While there have been some efforts to exert tighter control over finance, they have not fundamentally challenged the relations that this sector has established with other spheres of the economy over recent decades.

Financialisation is no epiphenomenon. It is a process that gets to the very heart of how contemporary capitalism is organised. Indeed, 'fictitious capital' has taken a central place in the general process of capital accumulation. Incarnated in debts, shares, and a diverse array of financial products whose weight in our economies has considerably increased, this fictitious capital represents claims over wealth that is yet to be produced. Its expansion implies a growing pre-emption of future production.

Fictitious capital's rising power results from substantial transformations in the financial sphere itself, as well as changes that have taken place in its relations with the rest of the social world – from the production of goods and services to nature, states and wage-labour. If finance develops according to a dynamic of its own, the hypothesis underpinning this book holds that the boom of fictitious capital is also the product of unresolved social and economic contradictions. As Fernand Braudel eloquently puts it, financialisation is a 'sign of autumn'.[1]

The development of high finance in fourteenth-century Florence responded simultaneously to both the new opportunities for profit to

---

1 Fernand Braudel, *Civilization and Capitalism, 15th–18th Century: The Perspective of the World*, Berkeley: University of California Press, 1984, p. 246.

be found in financing public debts and the erosion of profitability in the production and trading of textile products. Social inequalities grew as the commercial and productive activities that had allowed the great rise of a middle class began to disappear. Financial profits were now concentrated in the hands of a small financial elite.[2] In Venice, Genoa and then Amsterdam in the seventeenth century, 'The city's social oligarchy became inward looking', 'withdrawing ... from active trade, and tending to transform into a society of rentier-investors on the look-out for anything that would guarantee a quiet and privileged life.'[3] Financialisation, deindustrialisation and social polarisation marched in concert – and they signalled decline.

There are plenty of good reasons to think that contemporary financialisation marks a new autumn. First of all, since the 1980s we have seen a continuous rise in indebtedness in the main rich economies. Even though there are major disparities in the level and composition of the various countries' debts, the tendency is a clear and general one. A second striking phenomenon is the fact that the growth of the financial sector's share in the economy translates into a rise in financial profits' share of overall profits. A third phenomenon – and one that is now well documented – is the growth of inequalities. Particularly marked in the Anglo-Saxon countries, this change is apparent in all developed countries, with increased inequality of both incomes and assets.[4] Financialisation is directly implicated in this in two distinct ways: firstly, because it allows for a rise in the incomes associated with capital ownership (interest, dividends, capital gains on the stock markets, real-estate revenues); secondly, because it brings a rise in financial sector remuneration in terms of salaries.[5]

The last major factor to note is the marked tendency in all high-income countries for growth rates to slow (see Figure 1). This decline

2   Giovanni Arrighi, *The Long Twentieth Century: Money, Power, and the Origins of Our Times*, London and New York: Verso, 2010, p. 324.

3   Braudel, *Civilization and Capitalism*, pp. 266–7.

4   Thomas Piketty, *Capital in the Twenty-First Century*, Cambridge, MA: Belknap Press, 2013.

5   Olivier Godechot, 'Financialization is marketization! A study of the respective impacts of various dimensions of financialization on the increase in global inequality', MaxPo Discussion Paper, No. 15/3 (2015).

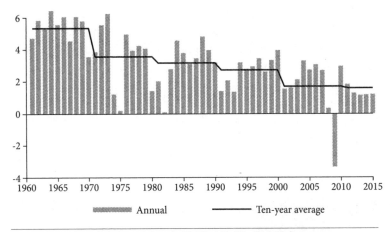

Source: Author's computations using World Bank World Development Indicators

Figure 1: GDP growth in high-income countries (per cent growth)

coincides with the decline of industrial activities in the richest countries and a reduction of these countries' share of the world economy. Whereas in 1990 the high-income countries produced 80 per cent of world GDP, by 2015 this figure had fallen to 64 per cent (World Bank-WDI).

Given these considerations, we can grasp how important it is to understand financialisation as a systemic phenomenon. But what exactly do we mean by 'financialisation'? The problem is linked to the plural uses of the concept, as well as the phenomenon's different aspects: the liberalisation of finance; the internationalisation and increased sophistication of financial markets; the growth of indebtedness among firms, households and states; the tendency toward the privatisation of social security systems and of nature; the fragmentation of the workers' movement; the proliferation of financial crises… Beyond this plurality then, does financialisation have any underlying structure that can explain the tendencies feeding what at first glance look like disparate events and processes?[6] The hypothesis examined

---

6   Here we are adopting the critical-realist epistemological approach. For an introduction to Roy Bhaskar's seminal, explicitly Marxian theory, Tony Lawson's derivation of it in the field of economics (*Economics and Reality*, London: Routledge, 1997), and the

in this book is that, even if financialisation has no unitary structure, there does at least exist a cluster of interdependent processes constituting it as a historical and spatial incarnation of the capitalist mode of production. The rising power of fictitious capital is the nodal point of this shift. If financialisation cannot be thought in isolation from the two other great markers of contemporary capitalism – globalisation and neoliberalism – it is above all distinguished by the accumulation of drawing rights over values that are yet to be produced.

The hypothesis associating financialisation with decline is not a self-evident one. Braudel himself referred to the success of financial capitalism in Europe between 1830 and 1860, 'when the banks took hold of everything, of industry and then the commodity, and the economy in general became strong enough finally to support this structure'.[7] According to Rudolf Hilferding, finance capital was at the heart of the lightning growth of German industrial capitalism at the turn of the twentieth century. For his part, Alexander Gerschenkron, the great theorist of 'catching up', explained that finance was a weapon in the arsenal of institutional tricks allowing a drive toward accelerated industrialisation, directly reaching large-scale production.[8] Financialisation was thus also the springtime of industrial capitalism. So, if today it marks the sign of autumn, we have to explain why that is the case.

What are the roots of contemporary financialisation? And, in turn, what tensions does it generate? In a 'Regulation School' perspective, a system pulled along by finance can be described as a set of mechanisms capable of temporarily containing the dissonances of accumulation. In their own very different or even radically opposed ways, Post-Keynesian and Hayekian approaches each point to a capitalist dynamic tormented and destabilised by inappropriate regulatory, budgetary and

---

implications for strategies for developing a critique of neoclassical economics, see B. O'Boyle and T. McDonough, 'Critical realism, Marxism and the critique of neoclassical economics', *Capital and Class*, 35:1 (2011), 3–22, and Ben Fine, 'Debating critical realism in economics', *Capital and Class*, 30:2 (2006), 121–9. For a discussion of the main critiques that have been formulated with regard to critical realism in the field of economics, see M. Da Graça Moura and N. Martins, 'On some criticisms of critical realism in economics', *Cambridge Journal of Economics*, 32:2 (2008), 203–18.

7   Fernand Braudel, *La dynamique du capitalisme*, Paris: Flammarion, 2002, pp. 65–6.

8   Alexander Gerschenkron, *Economic Backwardness in Historical Perspective*, Boston: Belknap Press of Harvard University Press, 1962.

monetary policies. For its part, the Marxist point of view privileges the contradictions and conflicts that undermine – and at the same time drive – a mode of production through its historical developments. From this perspective, the eruption of finance is nothing other than a manifestation of capitalism running out of breath, as evidenced by the succession of increasingly violent financial crises since the early 1980s.

These different points of view will inform our own rather pessimistic argument. The contemporary accumulation of fictitious capital is already caked with the frosts of winter. For a time, the increasing sophistication of finance allowed a certain concealment of the growing disconnect between, on the one hand, the exhaustion of the productive dynamic, and, on the other, the needs of capital and popular aspirations. The 2007–8 crisis stripped away the veil: austerity policies, structural reforms and the priority given to financial stabilisation seek to ensure that it is capital's needs and not the people's that prevail. Such is the basis for today's great social regression.

CHAPTER ONE

Beyond Greed

In public debate, the question of financialisation has primarily been posed in moral terms. Recent scandals resulting from revelations about ill-practice in the big banks have brought this sector into great disrepute. Here, we will not attempt to redeem a profession whose contribution to the common good we would justifiably consider inversely proportional to the astronomical remuneration it awards itself. But as we shall see, no attempt to explain the crisis in terms of the immorality of financial actors will stand up to analysis.

A WHIFF OF SCANDAL

In the very heart of Wall Street, the con artist Bernie Madoff played a trick as old as the world itself on a number of powerful financial institutions, namely the Ponzi scheme. This former tennis player hoodwinked Santander, HSBC, Natixis, Royal Bank of Scotland, BNP Paribas, BBVA, Nomura Holdings, AXA, Crédit Mutuel, Dexia, Groupama and Société Générale, among others (just like millions of Russian savers and hundreds of thousands of Albanians were duped after the fall of the socialist regimes – helping them discover the joys of capitalism!). The Madoff affair is symptomatic of an atmosphere of blind confidence in the capacities of financial valorisation. However, there was nothing sophisticated about it, nor any direct link with the US real-estate bubble of the 2000s. In his March 2009 legal deposition, Madoff admitted that his stratagem consisted of depositing his clients' money in the bank, and when they wished to withdraw it, he drew on the money in the 'bank account that belonged to them or other clients to pay the requested funds.'[1] All the same, this extreme chicanery – it was, after all, a matter of 17–20 billion dollars! – was just the tip of the iceberg of the fraud that was taking place. Indeed, in general it was the tricksters who got richest.

---

1 'Madoff trustee sues JPMorgan for $6.4 billion', reuters.com, 2 December 2010.

We can see that in the United States, on average and over time, neither small savers nor collective saving funds or pension funds are capable of realising profits through speculation. They cannot achieve capital gains superior to those corresponding to the movements of the market itself.[2] There is no stock miracle for employees who put their savings into shares in order to save for their retirement. Neoclassical financial theory sees this as a proof of financial markets' efficiency: indeed, its basic theorem stipulates that there is no possibility of arbitrage on the financial markets.[3] To put it another way, the level of financial remuneration is always identical to the degree of risk and the maturity of the asset concerned; or, in more simple terms, there is no 'money machine' for guaranteeing self-enrichment, for example by borrowing at a lower rate and lending at a higher one. And yet that is exactly what carry trade entails, for it consists of borrowing at low rates in one currency in order to invest at higher rates in another. This practice, as lucrative as it is widespread,[4] represents a mystery that standard financial theory is incapable of explaining, even when it does take into account the risks associated with the rare but abrupt variations in exchange rates.[5]

Of course, the neoclassical theorists of modern finance consider the behaviour of small shareholders erratic. Yet, in their view, the blips caused by the latter's errors are immediately corrected by the action of smarter financial agents capable of beating the market – that is, hedge funds earning a lot more money than the average market movements. These funds are supposedly superior thanks to their small and very highly paid teams: 'the greatest army of mathematicians, physicists and computer specialists ever brought together'.[6] It is true that hedge funds

---

2   Burton G. Malkiel, 'Returns from investing in equity mutual funds 1971 to 1991', *The Journal of Finance*, 50:2 (1995), 549-72; Terrance Odean, 'Do investors trade too much?', *The American Economic Review*, 89:5 (1999), 1279-98.

3   Stephen A. Ross, *Neoclassical Finance*, Princeton: Princeton University Press, 2009, p. 1.

4   Gabriele Galati, Alexandra Heath and Patrick McGuire, 'Evidence of carry trade activity', *BIS Quarterly Review*, 3 (2007), 27-41.

5   Òscar Jordà and Alan M. Taylor, 'The carry trade and fundamentals: nothing to fear but FEER itself', *Journal of International Economics*, 88:1 (2012), 74-90.

6   Augustin Landier and David Thesmar, *Le grand méchant marché: décryptage d'un fantasme français*, Paris: Flammarion, 2008, p. 29.

mobilise all means at hand; for example, at the beginning of the 2010s, they began using personal assistance software, modelled on that used by elite athletes, in order to

> help fund managers work out when they perform best. Do they make their best trades in the morning after two cups of coffee? Do they function better on their own in a quiet room rather than a big open-plan office, buzzing with people, or do they come back from a liquid lunch invigorated and inspired, ready to make their best decisions?[7]

The neoclassical theorists' approach often neglects one fundamental aspect, however: that, as in top-level sports, the quest for performance at any price has the corollary of cheating. Having the best analyses available and the best understanding of the financial dynamics at work is, certainly, essential to pulling off the most successful operations. Yet we can also employ the good old 'Huggy Bear method'. Even if this practice is illegal, access to private information is often key to one's fortunes on the finance markets, and all the more so when there is little chance of getting caught. Hedge funds, like the big merchant banks to which they are linked, are often in a position to benefit from exclusive access to information that allows them to beat the market. Even if the hypothesis as to the information efficiency of the financial markets has carried off a clutch of Nobel Prizes, in reality it is imperfect information that drives finance.[8]

From the Butner Federal Correction Complex where he is sitting out a 150-year prison sentence, Bernie Madoff – who was until recently non-executive president of the NASDAQ – explained in no uncertain terms: insider trading 'has been present in the market forever, but rarely prosecuted. The same can be said of front running of orders.'[9]

---

7 David Oakley, 'How to build a better active manager', FT.com, 15 September 2013.

8 As against the finance-market efficiency hypothesis, the Grossman-Stiglitz paradox argues that if a market is efficient from an informational point of view – if all the relevant information is contained in market prices – then no agent would have any motivation to acquire the information on which the prices are based. Yet if no one seeks out this information, then it is impossible for it to be revealed by the interactions of market agents.

9 'Madoff, in Christmas Eve letter, says insider trading has gone on "forever"', cnbc. com, 25 December 2012.

The crime of insider trading consists of engaging in transactions on stocks about which one has non-public information. 'Front running' involves exploiting one's knowledge of clients' past instructions in order to effect operations to one's own benefit, either in advance of, in parallel to, or immediately after these instructions.

Although it is by definition difficult to evaluate the extent of these practices, an empirical study has confirmed their existence. The research undertaken by Fang Cai looked into futures transactions on Treasury Bonds at the Chicago Board of Trade, the Chicago market specialising in futures operations, between 2 September and 15 October 1998. This was the period of the collapse and then bailout of the Long-Term Capital Management (LTCM) hedge fund.[10] In many regards, the LTCM case prefigured the problems encountered during the 2007–8 financial crisis. The board of the fund used complex mathematical methods for its operations – which in large part concerned derivative products – and its members included Myron Scholes and Robert Merton, two economists awarded the Nobel Prize in economics in 1997 for their contribution to financial theory and, more particularly, their determination of the value of derivative products. LTCM was also closely connected to the main investment banks on the New York exchanges. It was the fear of the chain reaction that would have resulted had LTCM gone bankrupt that led the New York FED to organise a salvage operation, to which fifteen major US and European banks contributed.

By the end of summer 1998, LTCM's financial difficulties were widely known. Also known was the fact that the fund had massively gambled on a fall in US Treasury Bonds. Unfortunately for LTCM, the Treasury Bond prices greatly increased. In an attempt to avoid considerable losses and reduce this unfavourable exposure, LTCM had no choice but to buy a huge quantity of bonds on the futures markets. Given the sums at stake, these transactions had a significant impact on stock prices. Cai's study manages to identify the orders given by LTCM and executed through the intermediary of the Bear Stearns bank. It

---

10   Fang Cai, 'Was there front running during the LTCM crisis?', International Finance Discussion Papers 758, Board of Governors of the Federal Reserve System, federalreserve. gov, February 2003.

shows that the agents charged with executing LTCM's orders did not simultaneously place orders in their own name in order to profit from the opportunity. So there was no front running in the strict sense. This was probably because the agents did not want to violate the rules established by the regulator in charge of the futures markets, and because they wanted to preserve their good relations with Bear Stearns, which placed LTCM's orders. Conversely, however, there was indeed front running in a wider sense. Since the futures market was at the time an open-outcry market, traders could interpret the noise, body language and hand signals of the agent in charge of LTCM's operations and thus place orders for their own accounts before the LTCM orders were given. This informational advantage is expressed in the data showing an abnormal level of transactions in the one to two minutes preceding the transactions linked to LTCM, which contributed to aggravating the fund's losses. Cai's study challenges the hypothesis that the agents who make the financial markets work at a micro-level do not have informational advantages. In fact, this type of asymmetry is found even in the most open public markets.

In the wake of the 2007–8 crisis, several scandals confirmed that this problem was not limited to the market's trading-floor operatives alone – far from it. They showed how the big banks and hedge funds had exploited their informational advantages. Thus, in 2013, SAC Capital – a $15bn hedge fund specialising in securities markets – was convicted of insider trading, having sold en masse its shares in two pharmaceutical companies, Wyeth and Elan, after becoming aware of the failure of tests into Alzheimer's treatments.[11]

Following the Abacus scandal, Goldman Sachs implicitly recognised that it had engaged in forms of front running. Abacus was the name of a complex product, a *mille-feuille* of subprime real-estate credit derivatives created by the Paulson & Co. hedge fund in 2006 and sold by Goldman Sachs to institutional investors for a total of over $10bn. In 2007 it was again Paulson & Co. that selected the loans for the new version of Abacus. Since the hedge fund had been at liberty to choose even the most fragile products, it was particularly well placed to know

---

11   Kara Scannell, 'SAC pleads guilty but judge stops short of accepting plea', FT.com, 9 November 2013.

that these products would collapse; it thus made a massive bet on these securities falling. However, Goldman Sachs did not inform its clients of the fact that Paulson was, indeed, behind the choice of the underlying loans, and even less that it had taken positions betting on their value falling.[12] This case well illustrates the way in which complex merchant banks/hedge funds dominate finance at the expense of other actors – in this case, pension funds and other banks. IKB, a German bank specialising in the long-term financing of small and medium-sized businesses, and which was at that time partly state owned, had to be bailed out with public money in August 2007.

During this affair, Goldman Sachs preferred to reach an agreement with the SEC (the US financial markets commission) and pay a $550m fine rather than go to trial. The fine amounted to around fourteen days of the bank's profits for that year. In contrast, the trader directly responsible for this product, Fabrice Tourre, was prosecuted and found guilty in summer 2013. His private email correspondence, revealed as part of the investigation, is extremely valuable in documenting the frame of mind of an actor directly implicated in producing the sub-prime crisis. At the beginning of 2007, a few months before the crisis broke, the young trader wrote that he was 'standing in the middle of all these complex, highly leveraged, exotic trades [he] created without necessarily understanding all of the implications of those monstruos-ities!!! [sic]'. Conscious that 'poor little subprime borrowers won't last long', he nonetheless sold bonds 'to widows and orphans'. Ironically, however, he stated that he was not 'feeling too guilty about this' – after all, 'the real purpose of [the] job is to make capital markets more effi-cient and ultimately provide the US consumer with more efficient ways to leverage and finance himself'.[13]

In a few lines, Tourre bluntly demonstrated the main virtue of the financial market efficiency hypothesis – namely, that it serves to justify the operations that bring colossal incomes to those who master the markets. The Abacus case moreover demonstrated that the role of the big investment banks and hedge funds is certainly not limited to cor-recting market distortions: it also consists of creating these distortions,

12   'The Goldman Abacus deal', sevenpillarsinstitute.org, 25 April 2011.
13   'Goldman helps fan interest in Tourre', documentcloud.org, April 2010.

in such a manner as to organise transfers of wealth. Despite the great pregnancy of the discourse on market efficiency, we arrive at what is altogether a rather prosaic conclusion: the institutions establishing themselves at the centre of the world's financial system use and abuse their position and the exclusive information available to them in order to make money.

Looking beyond these instructive examples, revelations that the world's biggest banks had mounted coordinated efforts to manipulate two essential financial markets – the money market and the currency market – affected the system's very foundations. In the first case, the scandal had to do with the fixing of inter-bank interest rates (LIBOR): between 2005 and 2009, the main banks had been able to mask their vulnerability by underestimating the effective rates. Even better, given that contracts worth many hundreds of thousands of billions of dollars are linked to LIBOR, the big banks could make considerable financial gains by playing with these minimal differences – and they did so for more than two decades.[14] The second case concerned the most important financial market: the currency market, with its daily exchange volume of some $5.3tn. Through coordinated movements over very short periods – less than 60 seconds – the big banks were able to manipulate the exchange rates of the main currencies to their own advantage.[15]

A 'FLEXIBLE' MORAL HAZARD

These scandals doubtless contributed to a moment of rationalisation in the financial markets and may lead to an improvement in their functioning, but they do not challenge those markets in any fundamental sense. So it is important to show that, even if greed and dishonesty did play a significant role in the crisis, the craze for sophisticated financial products and the financial bubble cannot be reduced to a question of individual morals or irresponsibility. At first glance, however, the subprime mechanism would seem to provide evidence in favour of that argument.

---

14   Douglas Keenan, 'Libor misreporting', informath.org, 12 February 2013.

15   Daniel Schäfer and Caroline Binham, 'Probes into forex trading spread across globe', FT.com, 1 November 2013.

Right at the bottom of the financial chain, we find the sale of real-estate credit to households – debts that serve as the raw material for derivatives products and which contributed to feeding the bubble. The sharp rise in securitisation makes it possible to detach distributing credit from exposure to credit risk. Those who distribute credit among households re-sell the debt on the financial market, at which point they are remunerated through the payment of a commission. Once the resale has been realised, they are no longer linked in any way to the borrowers – so they have no reason to concern themselves with the latter's capacity to repay the debt. The securitisation of credits leads to a slackening of inquiries into borrowers' financial situation.[16] Whereas borrowers are generally required to have assets and/or a regular flow of income, the United States in the 2000s saw a massive rise in NINJA loans: lending to those with 'No Income, No Job, no Assets'. Since the traditional channels of credit were saturated and institutional investors were hungry for derivatives products, the banks set out in search of new clients. For borrowers, the options on offer may have seemed rather tantalising. Judge as you may: certain contracts did not anticipate any checking of borrowers' resources; for the first ten years, the borrower only had to pay back interest; if they increased their total debt, they could also pay less than the monthly amount corresponding to the repayment of the interest and of the principal.[17] Capping all this, home ownership also allowed people to obtain further credit for consumer purchases.

Combined with aggressive marketing, these advantageous credit conditions brought a considerable number of lower-income households into financial circuits linked to real estate. Thus, in the United States, the proportion of households that owned their own home rose from 64 per cent in the mid-1990s to 69 per cent in the mid-2000s, pushing up prices. Credit was issued imprudently on the basis that a continual rise in prices would in any case allow for its reimbursement in cases of default, i.e. via foreclosures. Here we arrive at the

---

16   Benjamin J. Keys, Tanmoy Mukherjee, Amit Seru and Vikrant Vig, 'Did securitization lead to lax screening? Evidence from subprime loans', *The Quarterly Journal of Economics*, 125:1 (2010), 307–62.

17   Steven Pearlstein, '"No Money Down" falls flat', *Washington Post*, 14 March 2007.

fundamental explanation of the problem: this type of loan is a typical example of a 'moral hazard', when agents take an excessive risk but without fully bearing the consequences. Bankers and brokers are encouraged continually to provide loans because they pocket commissions at each level of the securitisation chain, at the same time as they completely offload the risk by selling these securities on the markets.

Such a system was, of course, unsustainable. The series of defaults saw the proportion of homeowners fall back down to 65 per cent in 2013, and millions of families who were pursued by their creditors had to abandon their homes. A small number opted to make strategic defaults on their mortgages: since prices were collapsing, it became increasingly advantageous to stop repaying their loans and return to rented accommodation.[18] According to one real-estate expert at the University of Arizona, this was the most advantageous option for numerous households in 2009–10, but they generally ruled it out because 'we have a double standard … individuals are told they have a moral obligation to pay their mortgages and corporations understand that contracts are to be breached when it's not economically efficient'.[19] Thus, the moral hazard is shared out unequally. While those selling credit could behave irresponsibly, distributing loans that they had every reason to think would not be repaid, for moral reasons indebted households often did not consider defaulting on mortgages that had become disadvantageous to them.

Without doubt, the idea of a 'flexible' moral hazard is well founded. As Fabrice Tourre's emails amply demonstrate – even beyond the particular case of Goldman Sachs – the big banks tried to limit their exposure to subprime securities and sometimes bet on them collapsing, even as they continued selling them to institutional investors. JPMorgan emerged victorious from the crisis: after having absorbed two of its rivals that were on the brink of bankruptcy, it became the largest US bank. However, in 2013 it faced numerous administration

---

18   Nonetheless, this option was much less open to them than it would have been under the previous regime, given the harsher regulations on personal bankruptcies signed into law by George W. Bush in 2005.

19   'How to strategically default on your mortgage and make life miserable for your bank', businessinsider.com, 17 October 2010.

inquiries over fraud, loss concealment, and shortfalls in implementing procedures to combat money laundering. The inquiries also concerned its failure to signal its doubts over Madoff's operations to the regulator. Two sets of proceedings were particularly striking in this regard, if only for the record penalties – over $13bn – resulting from the rulings.[20] The first concerned procedural errors and irregularities leading to the unwarranted foreclosure of thousands of homes. The second concerned the fact that, during the crisis, the bank continued to sell its securitised products containing loans, even when it knew that the borrowers were on the brink of default. It is difficult to discover anything more about this affair, however, because it was settled out of court. In the second case, after an Asian client filed a suit against Morgan Stanley, certain details came to light regarding what Wall Street knew about subprimes.[21] In 2005 Morgan Stanley managers became aware that something had gone wrong: one employee, mentioning the case of a borrower who claimed to be earning $12,000 a month as the 'operation manager [*sic*]' of a tarot-reading house, concluded that the loans that his company was being given to turn into securities were senseless. By early 2006, the bank had made up its mind on the real-estate market, deciding to speculate on a fall in the very securities it was offloading onto its own clients. By 2007, it was in the mood for joking: when its team sought a name for a subprime derivative being sold as 'safer than triple A', the ideas they came up with included 'Mike Tyson's Punchout', 'Nuclear Holocaust', 'Hitman', 'Subprime Meltdown' or, more plainly, 'Sack of Shit'.

SELF-INTOXICATION

Financial actors were caught in their own trap. The crisis did indeed take place, and the big banks were shaken. Had central banks and governments not mounted a titanic intervention they would have disappeared. All of them. Some of the more fragile were bought up by

---

20   Kara Scannell and Tom Braithwaite, 'JPMorgan reaches $13bn deal with US authorities', FT.com, 19 October 2013.

21   Jesse Eisinger, 'Financial crisis suit suggests bad behavior at Morgan Stanley', dealbook.nytimes.com, 23 January 2013.

rivals on the cheap. Others bounced back from their difficulties fairly rapidly, albeit only thanks to the public authorities taking action. There was considerable shock in Paris, as in all the major financial centres. Among other things, we might recall the €5bn loss that Société Generale blamed on Jérôme Kerviel, or the emergency merger of the Caisse d'Épargne and the Banques Populaire, designed to consolidate their investment branch, Natixis, whose stock lost 95 per cent of its value between 2007 and 2009. We thus see that the big banks had not anticipated the disaster.

The collapse of Lehman Brothers on 15 September 2008 marked the key date in the crisis. Created in the mid-nineteenth century, and the fourth biggest US investment bank, the bankruptcy of this venerable institution unleashed the financial earthquake of which we are all aware, leaving a completely paralysed world finance system on the edge of the abyss. Called before the US Congress's commission of inquiry into the financial crisis, Richard Fuld, Lehman's CEO and the chairman of its board, ruefully lamented that ultimately his was the only bank that the authorities did allow to collapse. He also offered his interpretation of the events that had led to this:

Lehman's demise was caused by uncontrollable market forces … Looking back, Lehman Brothers grew its business during a period of huge capital accumulation and easy access to liquidity and asset financing. During that time, Lehman Brothers' profitability and balance sheet grew accordingly.

In 2007, when the U.S. housing market began to show signs of weakening, Lehman Brothers and many of its competitors had already accumulated large positions in what were considered less liquid assets. Many market observers, including government officials charged with oversight of the financial markets, believed that the problems in the subprime residential mortgage market were and would be contained.

In retrospect, one can now see that as 2007 progressed, the weakening in the U.S. housing market was worse than predicted and spread to other sectors of the financial system.[22]

---

22   'Dick Fuld testimony: no apologies here', WSJ.com, 1 September 2010.

Fuld denied that he had any personal responsibility for this, instead pointing to a collective blindness in the face of the financial system's vulnerability. Alan Greenspan, head of the US Federal Reserve during the boom period, confessed to a similar error of judgement, albeit in a more personal manner: 'Those of us who have looked to the self-interest of lending institutions to protect shareholder's equity (myself especially) are in a state of shocked disbelief.'[23] We might think it a bit simplistic to bury one's own responsibilities like this, but there is no reason to imagine that greed somehow rules out blindness.

Was the crisis more the product of erroneous beliefs than deliberate dishonesty? Various empirically based works would support such an idea. For example, one particularly instructive study poses the following question: did those at the heart of the financial-real-estate complex – who were in charge of securitisation and who thus enjoyed a good knowledge of conditions in the real-estate market and the bubble that was forming – make better-informed investment choices? The study's authors examine the real-estate investment behaviour of 400 agents in charge of securitisation in banks, investment funds and companies issuing mortgages. They compare this to the behaviour of other agents who were equally rich but were either (in one group's case) financial analysts in the big firms or (in a second group's case) lawyers unconnected to the real-estate sector.[24] The results are very telling: the agents working in securitisation did not anticipate the bubble by selling more homes than the other agents before prices nosedived; they did not adopt a more prudent course in limiting their acquisition of new homes; and nor did they manage to enrich themselves more than did the others. Rather, we find that quite the opposite was the case. This suggests that the people most implicated in creating the bubble were particularly prone to erroneous beliefs.

We can draw two conclusions from this. Firstly, the individuals who work at the heart of Wall Street are not – any more than anyone else – rational and omniscient *homines œconomici*. Cognitive biases (exaggerated optimism, blindness in the face of disaster, conformism)

---

23   'Greenspan admits errors to hostile House Panel', WSJ.com, 24 October 2008.
24   Ing-Haw Cheng, Sahil Raina and Wei Xiong, *Wall Street and the Housing Bubble*, National Bureau of Economic Research, 2013.

informed their personal decisions as professionals. Secondly, and as a corollary of this, financial instability is not a moral problem that can be regulated by changing the incentives for individual workers in the sector, for example by imposing financial penalties on traders. Rather, what is at issue here is the very framework of liberalised finance that allows and encourages such behaviours.

THE DERIVATIVES FACTORY: BETWEEN THE PERFORMATIVITY OF ECONOMIC THEORY AND POLITICAL-IDEOLOGICAL WORK

Where does the liberalisation of finance come from? It is the fruit of multiple transformations of the sector, linked to national policy decisions, the development of the international context, and technological and organisational innovations. We can start by taking the example of derivatives products. Derivatives are instruments that allow certain economic actors to protect themselves against an asset's price variations by transferring the risk to speculators. The latter, for their part, hope to realise a profit by correctly anticipating price movements. The speculative side is particularly attractive because these financial products are totally shorn of the characteristics of the assets concerned, apart from one: the changes in their prices.[25] Since to possess a derivative product is to possess a financial exposure – that is, solely the future projection of the return on an asset – this means a rise in the power of finance. This is true almost even in the mathematical sense of the word 'power': there is a sort of 'finance to the power of two' corresponding to the massive rise in derivatives. Derivatives contracts allow an actor to take on a maximal risk exposure without committing much money.[26] Let us take an example. If you anticipate a rise in the price of oil, you can buy a barrel for €100 and stock it. Or you could buy a derivative on oil, allowing you to make the same bet but for only a few euros. In other words, derivatives products offer the possibility of taking an exposure on the price movements of twenty-five barrels of oil, using

---

25   Merton H. Miller, 'The derivatives revolution after thirty years', *The Journal of Portfolio Management*, 25:5 (1999), 10–15.

26   Dick Bryan and Michael Rafferty, 'Financial derivatives and the theory of money', *Economy and Society*, 36:1 (2006), 134–58 (p. 136).

the same amount it would take to buy just one barrel. This allows a reduction in the cost of covering price movements as compared to buying a real asset and, in correlation with this, makes speculation much less expensive.

The fact that risk-taking proliferated and spread across the whole financial system through complex derivatives products explains why the conjunctural reverse on the subprime markets resulted in a systemic financial crisis. The development of these products (to which we will return in Chapter 4) is extraordinary: having been negligible at the beginning of the 1970s, they were worth $865bn in 1987, before reaching a notional value of $685tn at the end of the 2000s. The enormous growth in derivatives is closely associated with the Chicago Board Options Exchange (CBOE). Opened in 1973, this market was one of the first modern derivatives product markets and the prototype for those that subsequently appeared in London, Frankfurt and Paris. In one fascinating paper, MacKenzie and Millo show how economic theory can be performative in a given historical context and how its mobilisation and appropriation by market actors can create economic operations with powerful consequences.[27]

Derivatives products – whether futures or options[28] – were an integral part of nineteenth-century finance. However, by the 1960s they were almost exclusively limited to derivatives on Chicago agricultural products, exchanged within the venerable Chicago Board of Trade (CBT), founded in 1848, and its competitor, the Chicago Mercantile Exchange (MERC). This agricultural derivatives sector was all the narrower in that prices were at that time subject to robust state control, reducing price fluctuations and limiting the interest in financial coverage. The reason for this marginalisation of derivatives was simultaneously both historical and moral. Financial regulation in the

---

27   Donald MacKenzie and Yuval Millo, 'Constructing a market, performing theory: the historical sociology of a financial derivatives exchange', *American Journal of Sociology*, 109:1 (2003), 107–45.

28   Futures are contracts through which one party commits to buying a definite quantity of a given asset from another party at a pre-established price on a given date. The asset concerned may be a raw material, but there are also futures on financial instruments and even stock indexes or interest rates. Options are contracts offering the possibility to buy or sell a given asset at a fixed date and for a fixed price, but without there being any obligation on the owner to exercise this option.

United States – regulation still heavily marked by memories of 1929 – remained hostile to derivatives products, which were associated with the wave of speculation that had led up to the Crash. Some of these contracts were also the object of a certain moral reprobation because they were seen as akin to gambling. A 1905 Supreme Court ruling thus banned all futures contracts that were not linked to some tangible asset. This prohibited any contract that could only be realised through the exchange of cash, such as a futures contract on a stock index.

The sector's prospects thus seemed rather gloomy. However, the leaders of the Chicago derivatives markets began working to clear the institutional hurdles blocking the development of these products. To this end, they employed individuals well embedded in the Washington political establishment. After Nixon came to power in 1969, they mobilised studies by economists to convince the new administration and the SEC to authorise the opening of a market dedicated to derivatives on financial products. One 1968 report drawn up by three Princeton economists had concluded that options enlarged the repertoire of strategies on offer to investors and were thus beneficial, 'just as the possibility of carrying an umbrella was an advantage to the pedestrian'.[29]

Three years later, another report would play a yet more important role. The then director of MERC, Leo Melamed, told one interviewer what happened:

> I met with [Friedman] in July [1971] and said 'I want to launch a futures market in currencies; do you think that's an ok idea?' He said, 'That's a terrific idea. I don't know how soon it will be viable because [exchange] rates are fixed, but it won't be too long before they are no longer fixed. You have to get a head start. It is a great idea, do it.' I said, 'Nobody is going to believe me,' so he said, 'Tell them I said so.' I said, 'I need it in writing,' and he said, 'You want a feasibility study on why currencies would make a good futures market?' I said, 'Exactly,' and he said 'I am a capitalist.' I said, 'How much?' So the study cost us $7,500 and that $7,500 is worth some $18 billion to the Merc today; it was a good trade. That was July. In August, Nixon closed the gold window

29   MacKenzie and Millo, 'Constructing a market, performing theory', p. 114.

and then of course all hell broke loose, and I knew fixed exchange rates were not going to last. ...

Presidents, financial ministers, central bankers who otherwise would not have allowed us near their doors, opened the door for us. It was magical! I met with Secretary of the Treasury George Shultz and sent Friedman's paper [ahead]. All he said was, 'If it is good enough for Milton, it is good enough for me.' His name was magic. After the launch, I met with every central banker in Europe and it was the same message: The great economist Milton Friedman thinks this is a great idea. And it worked.

Milton Friedman, the 1977 Nobel Laureate in economics, was the leader of the Chicago School. He would play a key role in breaking the hegemony of the Keynesians. His – rather simple – thesis rests on the idea that changes in the international financial order will create strong demand for coverage against the risks of change. For Friedman,

> It is highly desirable that this demand be met by as broad, as deep, as resilient a futures market in foreign currencies as possible in order to facilitate foreign trade and investment. Such a wider market is almost certain to develop in response to the demand. The major open question is where. The U.S. is a natural place and it is very much in the interests of the U.S. that it should develop here. Its development here will encourage the growth of other financial activities in this country, providing both additional income from the export of services, and easing the problem of executing monetary policy.[30]

Economics scholarship thus provided justifications that were decisively important to the creation of derivatives markets. But it did not achieve this on its own. There needed to be a context that would make sense of doing this (the dismantling of the Bretton Woods monetary system), and, following that, a collectively undertaken activity. The motives of the people who mobilised to create the derivatives markets were not those of strictly rational, self-interested *homines œconomici*.

---

30   Milton Friedman, 'The need for futures markets in currencies' [1971], *Cato Journal*, 31:3 (2011), 641.

Rather, their motives were constructed through a community in which direct and repeated interactions simultaneously allowed both cooperation and the punishment of those who tried to stand apart from this community.[31] Melamed offers a rather ironic idea of a mobilisation transcending individual interest when he explains his investment in the project carried forth by the small derivatives markets community. He admiringly evokes his father's involvement in the Bund, the socialist party of the Jews of eastern Europe,[32] explaining that it was his father who had taught him 'to work for society as a whole. My father had instilled in me [the] idea that you gain immortality by tying yourself up with an idea, or a movement, or an institution that transcends mortality.'[33]

If Melamed's cause won a decisive battle in the 1970s with the relaxation of the regulatory constraints on derivative products, only in the 1980s and 1990s would their usage become generalised and embrace other assets (like bonds) and other territories. In France, the deregulation of finance initiated in 1984 by the minister for economy and finance, Pierre Bérégovoy, and his chief of staff, Jean-Charles Naouri, resulted in the opening of first the MATIF (International Futures Market of France) in February 1986 and then, the following year, the MONEP (Traded Options Market). Both would be integrated into the London International Financial Futures Exchange (LIFFE) at the beginning of the 2000s.

Geographical expansion and the widened range of eligible assets were preconditions for the explosion of derivatives products in the 2000s. Gillian Tett, who follows this sector for the *Financial Times*, recounts this history in a lengthy study.[34] Importantly, she shows how,

---

31   Elinor Ostrom, 'Collective action and the evolution of social norms', *The Journal of Economic Perspectives*, 14:3 (2000), 137–58.

32   Leo Melamed and Bob Tamarkin, *Leo Melamed: Escape to the Futures*, New York: John Wiley & Sons, 1996, pp. 20–6.

33   Quoted by MacKenzie and Millo, 'Constructing a market, performing theory', p. 116.

34   Gillian Tett, *Fool's Gold: How Unrestrained Greed Corrupted a Dream, Shattered Global Markets and Unleashed a Catastrophe*, London: Abacus, 2010. More academic histories of derivatives also underline the imbrication of the performative dimension of economic theories and the political efforts of the dominant actors on these markets. See Bruce Carruthers, 'Diverging derivatives: law, governance and modern financial markets', *Journal*

at the turn of the 1990s, the US authorities began worrying about the rising power of derivatives products and, in particular, the fact that the banks were under no obligation to capitalise in order to cover these activities. In 1992 Mark Brickell – a former JPMorgan managing director of solid libertarian convictions – took the leadership of the International Swaps and Derivatives Association with the goal of resisting any intrusion by regulators.[35] The Group of Thirty – a very influential economics and monetary policy think-tank, at that time led by former FED president Paul Volcker – charged Brickell with drawing up a report aimed at influencing policy on this subject. This voluminous dossier, prepared by the JPMorgan derivatives team, came out in 1993. It proposed, on the one hand, evaluating risks on the basis of the available historical data (Value at Risk) and, on the other, evaluating actors' day-to-day exposure in function of prices on the securities market (Mark to Market). But its fundamental thrust was an appeal for the sector to be allowed complete self-regulation, and it sought to demonstrate that the industry was itself capable of strengthening stability by elaborating and adopting norms of its own. As Brickell hoped, the report's high level of technical detail greatly impressed the authorities concerned and put a stop to any intention they may have had of controlling such activities. Lobbying intensely throughout the 1990s, Brickell waged a merciless ideological battle against all those – notably in Congress – who wanted to regulate the industry, extending his alliances within the government machine under both Bush and Clinton. He was so successful that, until the 2007 financial crisis, the question had disappeared from the political agenda.

of Comparative Economics, 41:2 (2013), 386–400; Isabelle Huault and Hélène Rainelli-Le Montagner, 'Market shaping as an answer to ambiguities: the case of credit derivatives', *Organization Studies*, 30 (2009), 549–75.

35   The intensive relations between the big investment banks and regulators play an essential role in the construction of liberalised finance's institutional architecture. The Group of Thirty, which brings together central bankers, academics and bank executives, is the decisive site in the genesis of international finance regulation. Through the technical recommendations formulated in its authoritative reports, it serves as a channel between regulatory institutions and private financial lobbies like the International Swap and Derivatives Association and the Institute for International Finance. See the arguments of Céline Baud, *Le crédit sous Bâle II – un dispositif néolibéral de financiarisation en pratiques*, doctoral thesis, Jouy-en-Josas, HEC, 2013, Chapter 3, and Eleni Tsingou, 'Power elites and club-model governance in global finance', *International Political Sociology*, 8:3 (2014), 340–2.

Studies by economists played a legitimating role in each phase of the liberalisation of finance. This close connection was not without its ethical problems, since the economists in question often had a direct interest in promoting liberalisation. Such is the lesson of Charles Ferguson's film *Inside Job*, which notes for example that Larry Summers – former Harvard president but also a former Treasury Secretary in the Clinton administration and an adviser to President Obama – untiringly defended financial liberalisation throughout the 2000s, a period in which his ties with the finance industry brought him more than $20 million. In the wake of the financial crisis, a study of nineteen eminent financial economics specialists showed that, in addition to their university posts, most of them had affiliations with the private sector which they never publicly disclosed.[36] In France, too, a number of studies have added to the dossier on 'economists for hire'.[37] But again here, although there is indeed a conflict of interests, this is not the essential point. Once we have opened the Pandora's Box of liberalised finance, it is impossible to close it half way.

---

36 Jessica Carrick-Hagenbarth and Gerald A. Epstein, 'Dangerous interconnectedness: economists' conflicts of interest, ideology and financial crisis', *Cambridge Journal of Economics*, 36:1 (2012), 43–63.

37 Renaud Lambert, Frédéric Lordon and Serge Halimi, *Economistes à gages*, Paris: Les Liens qui libèrent, 2012; Jean Gadrey, 'Les liaisons dangereuses', alternatives-economiques.fr, 21 September 2009; Frédéric Lordon, 'Economistes, institutions, pouvoirs', blog.mondediplo.net, 21 November 2012; Laurent Mauduit, *Les imposteurs de l'économie*, Paris: J.-C. Gawsewitch, 2012.

CHAPTER TWO

Financial Instability

Credit growth is capitalism's Achilles heel.

James Tobin[1]

What went wrong? The short answer: Minsky was right.

Martin Wolf[2]

The simmering financial crisis boiled over in 2007. On 18 August the *Wall Street Journal* invoked the name of an economist it would now become rather attached to:

> The recent market turmoil is rocking investors around the globe. But it is raising the stock of one person: a little-known economist whose views have suddenly become very popular. Hyman Minsky, who died more than a decade ago, spent much of his career advancing the idea that financial systems are inherently susceptible to bouts of speculation that, if they last long enough, end in crises. At a time when many economists were coming to believe in the efficiency of markets, Mr. Minsky was considered somewhat of a radical for his stress on their tendency toward excess and upheaval. Today, his views are reverberating from New York to Hong Kong as economists and traders try to understand what's happening in the markets.[3]

Indeed, the post-Keynesian's name had already been circulating for some months among bank economists. In March, George Magnus published a study for UBS asking: 'Have we reached a Minsky

---

1 James Tobin, 'Review of *Stabilizing an Unstable Economy* by Hyman P. Minsky', *Journal of Economic Literature*, 27:1 (1989), 105–8.

2 Martin Wolf, 'The end of lightly regulated finance has come far closer', FT.com, 16 September 2008.

3 Justin Lahart, 'In time of tumult, obscure economist gains currency', WSJ.com, 18 August 2007.

moment?'[4] The *Financial Times*, the *Guardian*, and *Le Monde diplomatique* each devoted articles to the Levy Institute economist's analyses. Following this, heterodox economists invoked Minsky's name to try to defend their own interpretation of the crisis, as against the dominant tendencies in the discipline. To understand this craze for Minsky – but also to identify the limits of his approach – we must first outline his financial instability hypotheses.

THE INTRINSIC INSTABILITY OF FINANCE

Finance markets radically differ from markets for goods and services. Whereas in normal times rising prices weaken demand in the real economy, the opposite is generally true of financial securities: the more prices increase, the more these securities are in demand. The same applies the other way around: during a crisis, the fall in prices engenders fire sales, which translate into the acceleration of the price collapse. This peculiarity of financial products derives from the fact that their purchase – dissociated from any use-value – corresponds to a purely speculative rationale; the objective is to obtain surplus-value by reselling them at a higher price at some later point. Blinded to the disaster of the inevitable reverse, agents take on more and more debt in order to buy the assets that the bubble is forming around. Moreover, the self-sustaining price rise fuelled by agents' expectations is further exaggerated by credit. Indebtedness increases prices, and since the securities can serve as the counterpart to fresh loans, their increasing value allows agents to take on more debt. We find this same mechanism in most speculative episodes, from the seventeenth-century Netherlands[5] to the subprime crisis. In the former case, the speculation was on tulip bulbs; in the latter case, on residential properties.

The financial instability hypothesis allows us to inscribe these speculation dynamics in an understanding of economic cycles. Minsky sets out from the recognition that capitalist economies experience periods of acceleration and inflation and periods in which they are

---

4   Georges Magnus, 'The credit cycle and liquidity: have we arrived at a Minsky moment?', UBS Investment Research, 2007.

5   John Galbraith, *A Short History of Financial Euphoria*, London: Penguin, 1994.

caught in deflationary spirals in which debts become unsustainable. The 1960s and 1970s corresponded to the first dynamic and the 1930s (paradigmatically so) to the second, as described by the economist Irving Fischer in 1933. The latter dynamic comes about when economic agents trying to meet the deadlines on their debt repayments are forced to sell what they have at discounted prices. This brings a general downward movement in prices and diminished revenues, and ultimately leads to a growth in the weight of debt relative to income. This in turn unleashes a self-sustaining movement toward depression, which only state intervention can interrupt.

According to Minsky, this alternation of cycles cannot be explained by the play of real macroeconomic relations alone. Following Michal Kalecki, the post-Keynesian tradition supposes that, at the macroeconomic level, companies' profits flow from their own investment decisions ('the capitalists earn what they spend'). Minsky himself adopts this hypothesis, but suggests that it must be complicated by taking financial relations into account.[6] The past, present and future are linked not only by accumulated capital and labour power, but also by credit:

> the inherent instability of capitalism is due to the way profits depend upon investment, the validation of business debts depends upon profits, and investment depends upon the availability of external financing. But the availability of financing presupposes that prior debts and the prices that were paid for capital assets are being validated by profits. Capitalism is unstable because it is a financial and accumulating system with yesterdays, todays, and tomorrows.[7]

Credit relations are far from simple, for bankers and financial intermediaries are capitalists like any other: since they are in competition with one another and seek to make profits, they must constantly innovate. The result is a complex web of financial mechanisms that

---

6   Hyman P. Minsky, 'The financial instability hypothesis', in P. Arestis and M. Sawyer (eds), *The Elgar Companion to Radical Political Economy*, Cheltenham: Elgar, pp. 153–7.

7   Hyman P. Minsky, *Stabilizing an Unstable Economy*, New York: McGraw-Hill, 2008, p. 327.

separate the ultimate owners of wealth from the managers of the enterprises that control and exploit this wealth. Finance's tendency toward increased sophistication leads to three possible systems of relations between income and debts. The first corresponds to a situation in which economic actors' incomes cover their repayment obligations: thus, financial relations are solid and pose no problems to the overall reproduction of the economy. The second possibility is the establishment of speculative relations in which some economic units keep their debt rolling (they can only repay the interest, but not the principal). Such a configuration produces vulnerability, and the slightest conjunctural difficulty risks tipping the situation into the third possibility: the development of Ponzi structures, where income flows are insufficient to repay either the principal or the interest on the debt. The consequence is that indebtedness can only increase, ultimately leading to bankruptcies.

The stability of economies is largely dependent on the respective weights of these three types of financing relations. Minsky enjoys a certain posthumous renown because he emphasised that across periods of prolonged prosperity, economies gradually evolve toward a financing structure that makes the system unstable. Starting from a situation where financial relations covered by incomes are predominant, they move on to a situation in which speculative financial activities, and then Ponzi systems, become increasingly important, to the point that the insolvability of a small number of agents will end up provoking a collapse in asset prices. As Figure 2 shows, during periods of relative stability, the quest for profit leads to the development of financial innovations that accelerate credit circulation and reduce the quality of securities, which inevitably results in financial crisis or even a crisis in the real economy. Falling asset prices and the contraction of credit feed one another: agents in financial distress are forced to sell their holdings at whatever price they can; companies which are no longer able to obtain credit lay off staff, cut wages and lower the prices of their products; deflation leads to a growth in the weight of debts relative to incomes. Thus, the indebtedness of the euphoric period becomes ever less sustainable and threatens agents whose economic situation had up till then seemed solid.

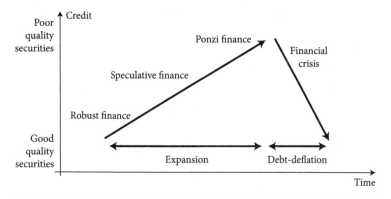

Source: Author's elaboration based on Minsky's ideas

Figure 2: Simple cycle of financial instability

THE PARADOX OF PUBLIC INTERVENTION

Financial crises do not always result in economic collapses like those of the 1930s.[8] Since the Second World War, the public authorities in the main capitalist countries have succeeded in avoiding a fresh Great Depression. They have done so by playing with two levers: on the one hand, the central bank acts as a lender of last resort, so as to limit chain-reaction bankruptcies and stabilise the financial markets; on the other hand, the state allows soaring public deficits and supports demand in order to offset the fall in investment and consumption – and, therefore, the fall in profits. Certainly, in recent decades, economic performance in the rich countries – taken as a whole, in terms of growth and employment rates – has been far from marvellous; 2009 saw the first contraction in the wealth produced worldwide since the Second World War. Europe even saw another fall in 2012–13. Nonetheless, economic policies have undeniably succeeded in their effort to keep the collapse under control: all the postwar financial crises – including the major shock of 2007–8 – have been contained. There has been no generalised depression as brutal as that of the 1930s.

Economic fluctuations are not, therefore, only the product of capitalist economies' internal dynamics, whether real or financial. They are

8   Hyman P. Minsky, 'Can "It" happen again? A reprise', *Challenge*, 25:3 (1982), 5–13.

also affected by the public authorities' intervention mechanisms. On the one hand, state action greatly reduces the risks of profits falling; on the other hand, it encourages expansionary phases.[9] Moreover, the authorities contribute to defining the control and organisation of the financial markets. Crucially, however, the regulator is not immune to the excessive optimism that economic actors can sometimes get caught up in. The relaxation of rules of caution makes it possible for the rate of financial innovations to accelerate. The result is that the longer the period of stability is, the greater the risks that are taken, and the greater the weakening of regulatory foolproofs.[10]

The interaction of the two levels of public intervention – the management of currency and budgetary expenditure, and the regulation and supervision of finance – allows us better to understand the onrush of financialisation that we have seen in recent decades. Indeed, the public authorities are all the more disposed to strip away financial regulations the more confident they are in central banks' and state budgets' capacity to contain financial crises. Meanwhile, for their part, financial operators are all the more inclined to take risks the more they know that the central bank will do everything to prevent a systemic risk becoming reality.

Figure 3 represents the paradox of government intervention. The effects of 'learning-by-doing' contribute to amplifying systemic risk. The memory of the Great Depression becomes ever more distant as capacities for crisis-management improve and financial actors as well as regulators become more optimistic. These expectations encourage financial innovation and looser regulation, both of which lead to an increasingly complex financial system. This growing sophistication allows the expansion of credit, at the cost of degrading the quality of securities. This, in turn, leads to small crises which are rapidly overcome thanks to the improved capacity to handle them. This cumulative dynamic produces a financial supercycle through which the accumulated risks become increasingly large – that is, the relative weight of speculative finance and Ponzi finance constantly increases – whereas,

---

9   Minsky, 'The financial instability hypothesis'.
10   Thomas I. Palley, 'A theory of Minsky super-cycles and financial crises', *Contributions to Political Economy*, 30:1 (2011), 31–46.

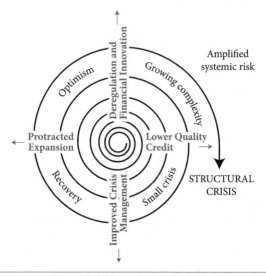

Source: Author's elaboration based on Minsky's ideas

Figure 3: The paradox of state intervention

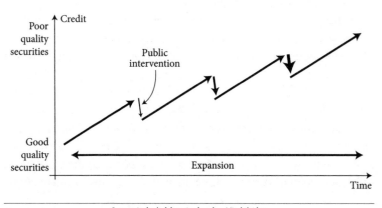

Source: Author's elaboration based on Minsky's ideas

Figure 4: Minskian financial supercycle

with each financial crisis, the public authorities have to devote even greater efforts to countering the depression spiral (Figure 4).

THE CONTEMPORARY FINANCIAL SUPERCYCLE

If we look at its narrowly financial logic, the great crisis of 2007–8 can be interpreted as the outcome of a financial supercycle. This is the argument supported by James Crotty in the *Cambridge Journal of Economics*:

> although problems in the US subprime mortgage market triggered the current financial crisis, its deep cause on the financial side is to be found in the flawed institutions and practices of the current financial regime … [This] New Financial Architecture refers to the integration of modern day financial markets with the era's light government regulation. After 1980, accelerated deregulation accompanied by rapid financial innovation stimulated powerful financial booms that always ended in crisis. Governments responded with bailouts that allowed new expansions to begin. These in turn ended in crises, which triggered new bailouts. Over time, financial markets grew ever larger relative to the nonfinancial economy, important financial products became more complex, opaque and illiquid, and system-wide leverage exploded. As a result, financial crises became more threatening. This process culminated in the current crisis, which is so severe that it has pushed the global economy to the brink of depression. Fear of financial and economic collapse has induced unprecedented government rescue efforts.[11]

The development of the finance markets since the 1970s thus results from the mutual reinforcement of two dynamics: on the one hand, the confidence placed in the self-regulation of the financial sector has opened the floodgates to financial innovation; on the other hand, the experiences of the 1980s debt crisis in the countries of the global

---

11 James Crotty, 'Structural causes of the global financial crisis: a critical assessment of the "new financial architecture"', *Cambridge Journal of Economics*, 33:4 (2009), 563–80 (p. 564).

South, the 1987 market crash in the US, the 1994 Mexican crisis, the Asian and Russian crises of 1998 and the 2001 crisis in the new economies have fed the sentiment that the authorities will be able to contain catastrophes.

The actions of Alan Greenspan, FED president from 1987 to 2007, did much to give credence to this belief. The measures taken to save LTCM in 1998, and then the heavy interest rate cuts following the bursting of the dotcom bubble in 2001, comforted market actors in their conviction that the FED would always intervene to contain their losses. This idea has also been associated with the concept of a 'Greenspan put'. The notion of the 'put' – borrowed from the vocabulary of option contracts – emphasises an implicit central bank support for financial values, equivalent to a 'put' option: that is, a guarantee that the price of financial assets cannot fall beneath a certain level. Indeed, in reducing interest rates, the FED supported asset prices: with lower interest rates, investors could take on more debt, at less cost, and invest in the stock markets. Moreover, returns on financial securities became more advantageous relative to the interest rate.

This asymmetrical monetary policy – which limits the fall in stock prices but places no barriers to their rise – has led financial actors to take greater risks. This is all the truer when it is combined with an active budgetary policy. Figures 5 and 6 show how monetary and budgetary policies have come to the aid of stock prices and, in the 2000s, of real estate. They show how these policies helped prices to recover rapidly in the few years following the financial collapse. If the budget deficit fell as the markets took off at the end of the 1990s, monetary policy, conversely, remained accommodating; in the 2000s, both of these levers were pulled simultaneously, indeed forcefully so after the 2001 crash, encouraging not only market recovery but also the expansion of the real-estate bubble.

The belief in the robustness of the financial system grew at a similar pace – all the more so given that the proliferation of exotic financial products seemed to promise a better dispersion of risks. Symptomatically, in July 2007, even as the first manifestations of the crisis were appearing, some proclaimed that 'There [would] be no Big Crash' because 'the finance industry has undergone genuine revolutions since

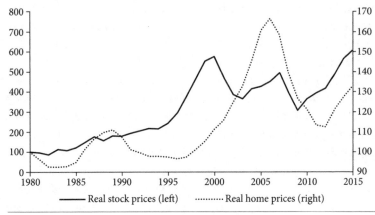

Source: Author's computations using Robert Schiller database

Figure 5: US stock and home prices (1980 = 100)

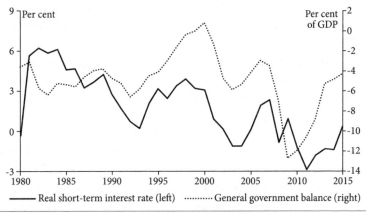

Source: Author's computations using OECD Indicators

Figure 6: US fiscal balance and real interest rate

the late 1990s: its resistance against trend turnarounds has improved, reducing systemic risks'.[12]

The 2007–8 crash saw the adoption of public crisis-containment policies operating on an unprecedented scale. In the United States,

---

12   Augustin Landier and David Thesmar, 'Le mégakrach n'aura pas lieu', lesechos. fr, 27 July 2007.

interest rates were reduced to zero and the budget deficit rose to close to 12 per cent of GDP in 2009. Budgetary and monetary policies in the other developed countries also developed in a similar direction, although they were generally rather less energetic.

Given the extent of the threat posed, other instruments were also mobilised, such as the recapitalisation and partial or total national-isation of banks and insurance companies, as well as new channels facilitating and expanding the supply of liquidity across different banks. Monetary policy also ventured into unknown territories: for example, the quantitative easing first implemented by the Bank of England and the FED led these institutions to buy hundreds of bil-lions of dollars' worth of government bonds and mortgage products in order to keep overall interest rates at very low levels (see also Chapter 6). These policies may not have brought about any major recovery in the real economy, but they did halt the fall in real-estate prices and allowed a strong rise in stock prices: in 2013 US equities caught up with their pre-crisis level. Moreover, low interest rates encouraged investors to purchase riskier securities (like bonds issued by fragile companies, or even the public debt of developing countries) in order to achieve a return. In short, the policies adopted in response to the crisis certainly did limit financial losses, but they also contributed to increasing risk-taking, and thus to heightening the systemic risk, in turn preparing the ground for the next financial catastrophe.

Neoclassical literature has grasped this problem by mobilising the notion of the 'meta-moral hazard'[13] or 'systemic moral hazard'.[14] This generalises the 'too big to fail' principle to all the actors involved in the system. In this reading, not only major institutions but financial actors in general tend to take excessive risks because they know that the public authorities will intervene to limit their losses.

The belief that the public authorities will take effective action when catastrophes occur is not mutually exclusive with the hypothesis that exaggeratedly optimistic forecasts will lead to an underestimation of

---

13   Marcus Miller, Paul Weller and Lei Zhang, 'Moral hazard and the US stock market: analysing the "Greenspan Put"', *The Economic Journal*, 112:478 (2002), 171–86.

14   Emmanuel Farhi and Jean Tirole, *Collective Moral Hazard, Maturity Mismatch and Systemic Bailouts*, National Bureau of Economic Research, 2009.

risks.[15] Moreover, we do not have to imagine a set of hyper-rational and opportunist economic agents taking advantage of implicit state guarantees in order to understand the cumulative effects when over-optimistic forecasts combine with the obligation on the authorities to intervene to avert systemic collapse. This was why Minsky's contribution proved fundamental to understanding the properly financial dynamic that led to the crisis of 2007–8.

THE INSTRUMENTAL USE OF MINSKY

Some of Minsky's works proved remarkably prophetic. Such was the case with a 1987 note of his devoted to securitisation. In this text, he showed that this financial technique 'implies that there is no limit to bank initiative in creating credit' and that the forces of financial globalisation could connect with the forces of the mortgage market.[16] Nonetheless, he did not draw from this the full set of conclusions that ought to have led him to revise his theoretical framework.

Indeed, the surge in speculation did not take place where his canonical model supposed it would (that is, in the disproportionate extension of credit to non-financial firms engaging in ultimately unprofitable investments). As we shall see in Chapter 4, the historical sequence in rich countries was characterised not by booming investment, but, on the contrary, by its decline, except during a short period in the second half of the 1990s which ended with the bursting of the dotcom bubble. Spiralling indebtedness appeared not in the productive sector but in households, states, and above all in the financial sector itself. This is a blindspot of Minsky's analysis, in large part flowing from the historical context in which it took form.

A second problem – perhaps a more serious one, and in any case a more political one – is the use to which Minsky's works have been put in handling the crisis.[17] To the extent that a financial crisis manifests

---

15   Xavier Ragot, 'Les banques centrales dans la tempête – pour un nouveau mandat de stabilité financière', in 5 crises. 11 nouvelles questions d'économie contemporaine, Paris: Albin Michel Éditions, 2013, p. 384.

16   Hyman P. Minsky and L. Randall Wray, Securitization, Levy Economics Institute, 2008.

17   Maria N. Ivanova, 'Marx, Minsky, and the Great Recession', Review of Radical Political Economics, 45:1 (2013), 59–75.

itself through a drastic reduction in liquidity (that is, the lack of buyers for financial securities), the only two means of halting the crisis are, on the one hand, exceptional refinancing by the central bank, or, on the other hand, an increase in the government bonds in circulation (indeed, these can be used as collateral for new loans and thus encourage a credit revival). These two mechanisms require that the central bank and the government 'validate' the structure of the liabilities generated by financial innovations and boom-era speculation in order to prevent a depression. While this policy did indirectly contribute to halting the rise in unemployment, its more immediate effect was to accelerate the rise in inequalities, thanks to the rebound in stock values and the rise in the salaries and bonuses linked to firms' now drip-fed profits. Thus, in the United States, the richest 1 per cent hoarded some 95 per cent of profits between 2009 and 2012; in the same period, the incomes of the 99 per cent stagnated (+0.4 per cent) whereas the 1 per cent's incomes jumped 31.4 per cent.[18]

Even if Minsky's intention was not to defend the enrichment of finance at the expense of the rest of society, he did nonetheless provide it with a comfortable means of extracting itself from the debacle it had inflicted on itself, without having to take responsibility for it. This helps us understand why financial commentators were so enthusiastic about his analyses when they needed to justify the exorbitant salvation plans. The crisis solutions superficially inspired by Minsky led to the socialisation of the costs of the financial collapse – indeed, on a scale never previously imagined – without the working classes or the unemployed ever feeling the supposed benefits of this 'communism for capital'. We should remember the significant sums involved: between autumn 2008 and the beginning of 2009, the total amount that states and central banks in the advanced countries committed to supporting the financial sector (through recapitalisation, nationalisation, repurchasing assets, loans, guarantees, injections of liquidity) has been evaluated at some 50.4 per cent of world GDP![19]

---

18   Emmanuel Saez, 'Striking it richer: the evolution of top incomes in the United States (updated with 2011 estimates)', University of California-Berkeley Working Paper 2013, pp. 1–8.

19   'Fiscal implications of the global economic and financial crisis', *IMF Staff Position Note*, No. SPN/09/13 (June 2009), p. 7.

Ultimately, what Minsky's analysis leaves partly unexplained is the very status of financial value. In the interests of shedding some light on this point, we will now bring into play the notion of fictitious capital.

CHAPTER THREE

Fictitious Capital: The Genealogy of a Concept

Finance is not somehow suspended above the real economy. On the contrary, it develops in relation with this economy and contributes to its transformations. Even if finance remains at some remove from the world of producing and trading commodities, it is part and parcel of the process of capital accumulation. It has a certain autonomy, but only in relative terms. Here we have a fundamental tension whose nodal points, vanishing lines and reconnection circuits we should try to identify more specifically. André Orléan's demonstration of finance's fundamentally two-sided character can serve as a point of departure for our considerations. Building on his very detailed analysis of the play of interdependences on the financial markets, Orléan describes the logic of a speculation rationality characteristically bringing about and feeding bubbles. Even so, 'mirroring strategies'[1] – strategies determined by agents' opinion of the opinion that agents in general will have of the opinion of agents in general, etc. - do converge toward a financial convention that is not simply unconstrained. It 'must rest on convincingly, properly argued considerations … It requires some minimal plausibility from the perspective of the fundamentals.'[2]

The price of financial assets is thus disputed between two poles: the autonomous dynamic of speculation and a loose but necessary relation with their fundamental value. However, the speculative logic is not the equivalent of the fundamental logic. While the former is elaborated in the game of mirrors of financial subjectivities, the latter has an underlying existence of its own which agents must always maintain a grip on. The process of valorisation through social production over-determines the process of financial valorisation. In other words,

---

1 André Orléan, *Le pouvoir de la finance*, Paris: Odile Jacob, 1999, pp. 67–74.

2 Ibid., p. 88.

speculative valorisation and fundamental valorisation are not symmetrical, for while speculation does necessarily refer to the process of valorisation through social production, the inverse is not the case. Yet that is the very thing the financial community tries to achieve by way of liquidity.

The liquidity that the financial markets work to organise has the objective of ensuring that the bets investors make on the future valorisation process can constantly be transformed into immediately available value. However, this ambition runs up against a 'fallacy of composition'. Even if each individual actor can offload the securities he holds, that cannot be true of all investors all at once. Keynes clearly demonstrated this point, stating that 'there is no such thing as liquidity of investment for the community as a whole'.[3] There is a simple explanation for this: the productive capital that has been invested, and the relations of indebtedness that underlie financial securities, do not represent immediately available value. They are promises. So it is only possible to sell them if someone else agrees to take them over.

What Orléan calls the paradox of liquidity starkly underlines the *relative* character of finance's autonomy. He uncovers the tension between the process of real valorisation and the process of financial valorisation – a tension at the heart of the questions raised by financialisation. Fictitious capital is the most adequate concept for dealing with this difficult problem. We will firstly identify its genealogy, before going on in the next chapter to describe the development of the basic and sophisticated forms that this category assumes in contemporary economies.

The concept of fictitious capital is today largely forgotten. Removed from *Palgrave* – the economics reference dictionary – in the 1990s, it is nonetheless a concept associated with two major thinkers, namely Friedrich Hayek and Karl Marx.

---

3   John Maynard Keynes, *The General Theory of Employment, Interest and Money*, London: Macmillan, 1936, p. 155.

The Austrian approach: fictitious capital
as an illusion and diversion of resources

You must save to invest, don't use the printing press
Or a bust will surely follow, an economy depressed.
'Fear the Boom and Bust', a Hayek vs. Keynes rap anthem[4]

For liberal writers, the production of fictitious capital means the monetary creation of capital by way of the credit system, without any counterpart on the terrain of real resources. It is an eminently pejorative term, with a whiff of the scam of constantly using new loans to maintain a facade of being able to pay off old ones.[5]

The notion first appeared in a treatise on monetary questions written by Charles Jenkinson, Earl of Liverpool, addressed to King George III and published in 1805. It appeared in a chapter in which Jenkinson sought to warn the sovereign against the serious risks posed by the proliferation of paper money. Context is important here. In 1797, uncertainties linked to the British crown's war against revolutionary France had forced the Bank of England to suspend the convertibility of its notes for gold and to issue small notes of £1 and £2: up until that point, notes had been used for major sums only, and the bearer could convert them. Jenkinson was thus worried by the risks of unregulated currency issuance becoming fragmented. Indeed, when the ordinary banks issued an excess of paper money, its value eroded and there was a wave of bankruptcies. The Bank of England was thus forced to intervene to preserve the integrity of the payments system. It was faced with the following dilemma: either to mint, at a loss, coins whose metallic value was higher than their face value – with the risk that they would immediately get melted into bullion and exported in this form, thus disappearing from domestic circulation; or else to stop converting

---

4 'Fear the Boom and the Bust' is a video portraying a rap battle in which characters representing Keynes and Hayek face off with their opposing arguments. Russell David 'Russ' Roberts, who participated in creating the video, is a Stanford economist devoted to propagating the Austrian School's neoliberal arguments among the general public. The video, which came out in 2010 and has been watched by more than four million people, can be viewed on YouTube.

5 Suzanne De Brunhoff, 'Fictitious capital', in *The New Palgrave Dictionary of Economics*, London: Palgrave, 1990, pp. 3409–10.

notes into metal and prop up circulation by issuing its own notes, at the risk of undermining its own credibility.

If Jenkinson's argument seems to be limited to the question of paper money, in fact he also had rather broader concerns in mind. We can see as much from the passage in which the concept of fictitious capital first appears:

> It seems to have been discovered of late years in this country, that, by a new sort of alchemy, Coins of Gold and Silver, and almost every other sort of property, may be converted into Paper; and that the precious metals had better be exported, to serve as capital, to foreign countries, where no such discovery has yet been made. But this new sort of *fictitious capital*, thus introduced within the kingdom, has contributed more than any other circumstance to what is called over-trading; that is, rash and inconsiderate speculations, and what is almost a necessary consequence, unworthy artifices to support the credit of adventurers already ruined, as well as other evils, which tend to corrupt the morals of the trading part of the community, and to shake the credit on which not only Paper currency, but the internal commerce of the kingdom is founded. In every commercial system, capital is certainly a necessary ingredient: but the prosperity of the British commerce depends not singly on capital; it depends still more on the good faith, honour, and punctuality of British merchants, for which they are so justly celebrated.[6]

He focused on paper money not only because it was replacing gold and silver coinage, but also because it came to represent 'almost every other source of property'. For Jenkinson, the fact that the notes substituting for money could correspond to various underlying assets represented a source of instability. He moreover made reference to John Law's money system – pledged against real-estate values and subsequently against the entire resources of the kingdom of France – whose speculative expansion resulted in the resounding collapse of

---

6   Charles Jenkinson, *A Treatise on the Coins of the Realm in a Letter to the King*, London: Effingham Wilson, Royal Exchange, 1880, p. 255 (italics added).

the Mississippi Company in 1720.[7] In substance, Jenkinson was thus arguing in favour of the gold-standard monetary system in which the entire supply of paper money has a counterpart in metal reserves. Yet what is notable in this extract is that Jenkinson was not only worried about the risk of paper money bringing devaluation; he also put his finger on the fictitious character of the capital that it allowed to be circulated. In sum, desperate financing and speculation threatened the moral integrity of the British trading system – and, ultimately, its prosperity – due to the circulation of inauthentic capital. If Jenkinson did not explicate its mechanisms, he clearly did have an intuition as to the dysfunction that fictitious capital introduced.

Why speak of fictitious capital? Numerous nineteenth-century economists worked to refine this point, and their reasoning would serve as the basis for the elaborations of neoliberalism's most important theorist, Friedrich Hayek. The first stage consisted of making explicit the link between issuing currency and extending credit.

Lord Lauderdale stated in an 1811 letter that 'by the same act with which a bank increases the circulating medium of a country, it issues into the community a mass of *fictitious capital*, which serves not only as circulating medium, but creates an additional quantity of capital to be employed in every mode in which capital can be employed'. His correspondent Dugald Stewart took this analysis a step further: 'The radical evil, in short, seems to be, not the mere over issue of notes, considered as an addition to our currency, but the anomalous and unchecked extension of credit, and its inevitable effect in producing a sudden augmentation of prices by a sudden augmentation of demand.'[8] The excess of credit produced by fictitious capital had a very real effect on prices.

In 1819, a House of Lords commission asked David Ricardo whether the fictitious capital resulting from an abundant circulation of paper money stimulated economic activity. Consistent with his hypothesis as to the neutrality of money, Ricardo responded in the negative, 'I do not think that any Stimulus is given to production by the

---

7   Galbraith, *A Short History of Financial Euphoria.*
8   Dugald Stewart, *Lectures on Political Economy. Vol. I. Appendix II.—: To B. II. Ch. ii.*, Edinburgh: Sir William Hamilton, 1855 (italics added).

Use of *fictitious Capital*, as it is called.' However, he conceded that, on rare occasions, it could encourage capital accumulation by increasing profits at the expense of wages.[9]

This grudging concession pointed to an essential theoretical problem that Hayek would later tackle head-on. He took as his point of departure a position that was widespread in the nineteenth century: that 'trade and financial crises are produced by an excess of consumption, not an excess of production'.[10] He therefore had to show that the 'central point of the true explanation of crises' was the 'phenomenon of a scarcity of capital making it impossible to use the existing capital equipment'.[11] Hayek accepted that this may seem a surprising proposition: 'That a scarcity of capital should lead to the existing capital goods remaining partly unused, that the abundance of capital goods should be a symptom of a shortage of capital, and that the cause of this should be not an insufficient but an excessive demand for consumers' goods, is apparently more than a theoretically untrained mind is readily persuaded to accept.'[12] But the paradox is only an apparent one. This relates to the role of fictitious capital, here considered as an excess of credit as compared to savings.[13]

The overabundance of credit distributed to capitalists translates into the rollout of an excessive number of production projects relative to the available resources. This results in a shortfall in the intermediate goods necessary for setting the purchased capital goods in motion.

What is commonly meant by over-investment is not an excess of investment relative to the demand for the ultimate product, but an

9   Jacob Viner, *Studies in the Theory of International Trade*, London: George Allen & Unwin, 1955, pp. 214–15 (italics added).

10   Y. Guyot, *La science économique*, Bibliothéque des sciences contemporaines, C. Reinwald, 1887.

11   Friedrich Hayek, *Profits, Interest, and Investment*, Clifton: Kelley, 1975, p. 149.

12   Ibid.

13   This problem of credit exceeding savings is often arrived at by way of the notion of forced saving, not only in Hayek but also in the writings of numerous other authors including Malthus, Walras and Schumpeter. Keynes also mentions it, indicating – following Bentham – that for him this notion only made sense in the context of full employment (*The General Theory of Employment, Interest and Money*, pp. 102, 104).

excessive launching of new undertakings which need for their completion or utilisation more capital than is available; in other words, "over-investment" implies not too much saving but too little.[14]

Figure 7 offers a summary portrayal of the destabilising effects that can result when credit not compensated by a rise in savings creates demand for additional investment assets. Crisis breaks out because there is insufficient capital – that is, unconsumed resources – to allow for the deployment of new facilities. This can only be resolved in two ways: either through the abandonment of production projects, making it possible to restore a correspondence between intermediate-goods needs and the available productive capital stock, or else by reducing consumption, thus allowing resources to be freed up to satisfy the need for intermediate goods. For Hayek, re-establishing an equality between savings, credit and new capital is indispensable to the harmonious usage of available resources.

This argument is rooted in the business-cycle theory that Hayek elaborated in the early 1930s. This theory gave rise to a very lively controversy with Keynes and Sraffa in the pages of *The Economic Journal* in 1931 and 1932. The exchange soon clearly turned

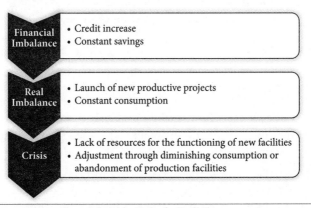

Source: *Author's elaboration based on Hayek's ideas*

Figure 7: From excessive credit to over-investment: the destabilising character of fictitious capital, according to Hayek

---

14   Hayek, *Profits, Interest, and Investment*, p. 167.

against Hayek. His attempt to combine Wickell's notion of natural interest rates – conceived as a way of thinking about barter economies – and Walras's notion of general equilibrium in the context of a monetary economy was full of logical contradictions and totally out of phase with the urgent economic demands of the time. Indeed, at that very moment this type of argument over the insufficiency of savings inspired Chancellor Brüning's disastrous deflationary policy which precipitated the coming to power of Adolf Hitler.

Nothing can salvage Hayek's early business-cycle theory: indeed, in later decades, even he distanced himself from it. But, when he identifies the excess of credit as a possible cause of crisis on account of its capacity to destabilise relative price levels, he points to a problem crucial to the questions that interest us here. What we should hold onto is the idea that credit not compensated by savings will not ultimately translate into accumulated capital. The stimulus provoked by the creation of fictitious capital is nothing more than illusion and waste, for it implies that part of the capital committed to production is instead diverted into other less efficient uses.

Marx's approach: the ambivalence of the forms of anticipating capital valorisation

> everything in this credit system is duplicate and triplicate, and is transformed into a mere phantom of the mind
>
> Marx, *Capital*, Vol. III, Chapter 29[15]

To my knowledge, Hayek makes no reference to the Marxist analysis of the concept of fictitious capital. This is no great surprise, given that, for the majority part of his life, he was a hardened anti-socialist. However, since he had assiduously frequented pre-1914 Austrian social-democratic circles, he was doubtless aware that Marx himself picked up on the idea – widespread among his contemporaries – that the credit money which bankers created out of nothing was a fictitious capital, frequently resulting in the wildest speculation.[16]

---

15   Karl Marx, *Capital*, Vol. III, Harmondsworth: Penguin, 1981, p, 603.
16   See Karl Marx, *Capital*, Vol. III, Harmondsworth: Penguin, 1981, pp. 525–42. For an

But Marx's judgement on the credit system was very different to Hayek's. For him, far from running up against the limits of the available resources, credit could overcome the barriers constituted by self-financing and the production of precious metals. It thus 'accelerates the material development of the productive forces and the creation of the world market'.[17] The idea of resource constraints was not completely missing here, but it was limited to those situations where the credit system 'appears as the principal lever of overproduction and excessive speculation in commerce' because here it forces 'the reproduction process, which is elastic by nature ... to its most extreme limit'.[18]

> The credit system has a dual character immanent in it: .... it develops the motive of capitalist production ... and restricts ever more the already small number of the exploiters of social wealth ... On the other hand however it constitutes the form of transition towards a new mode of production. It is this dual character that gives the principal spokesmen for credit .... Their nicely mixed character of swindler and prophet.[19]

Consistent with what was commonly accepted in the nineteenth century, for Marx fictitious capital does indeed result from the development of the credit system.[20] The exchange of loan-capitals is a means of valorisation de-correlated from the productive activity that gives rise to fictitious capital. Its constituent parts are the making available of loanable funds, repayment deadlines, and the corresponding

---

introduction to Marx's approach to fictitious capital see François Chesnais, 'La prééminence de la finance au sein du "capital en general", le capital fictif et le mouvement contemporain de mondialisation du capital', in *La finance capitaliste*, Actuel Marx Confrontations, Paris: PUF, 2006.

17   *Capital*, Vol. III, p. 572.
18   Ibid.
19   Ibid., pp. 572–3.
20   Robert Guttmann, 'Les mutations du capital financier', in François Chesnais (ed.), *La mondialisation financière*, Paris: Syros, 1996, pp. 76–7; Suzanne De Brunhoff, *La monnaie chez Marx*, Paris: Éditions sociales, 1967, p. 144. Lapavitsas sharply distances himself from Marx when he states that there is nothing inherently fictitious about loan capital (Costas Lapavitsas, *Profiting Without Producing: How Finance Exploits Us All*, London: Verso, 2013, p. 29).

interest. Nonetheless, fictitious capital is not reducible to the credit system alone. Marx's main original intuition was that the creation of fictitious capital proceeds from a more general logic of anticipating the capital valorisation process. Fictitious capital thus appears as a claim and a projection made by capital-holders; its failure leads to financial crises and social and political battles over the distribution of the resulting fallout.

In its various institutional incarnations, finance is essentially reducible to the advance of a certain monetary value in exchange for a promise of reimbursement or, indeed, a property title over activities that will create values as they play out. Finance thus establishes a mode of capital valorisation that seems to give money magical faculties. What Marx says about interest-bearing capital is also true of finance in general: 'it becomes as completely the property of money to create value, to yield interest, as it is the property of pear-trees to bear pears.'[21] The comforting idea that it is possible to separate the valorisation process from the production process and the exploitation of labour is a chimera, but it sustains what are for capital powerful mechanisms of domination.

How does the creation of fictitious capital work? 'The formation of fictitious capital is known as capitalization':[22] that is, it produces debts or securities whose value results from the capitalisation of the anticipated revenues.[23] As such, the central problem fictitious capital poses is not – as the Austrian school approach has it – the existence of prior savings sufficient to allow the creation of supplementary capital. The problem is that fictitious capital pre-empts the future valorisation process even as it makes it invisible. If, according to the Austrian approach, fictitious capital is synonymous with failure and wastage, in the Marxist analysis its fictitious character is not synonymous with the success or failure of the future valorisation process, even though it does indicate its fragility. In short, it poses the present valorisation

---

21   Marx, *Capital*, Vol. III, p. 516.

22   Ibid., Vol. III, p. 597.

23   The calculation of its realisation can be expressed in the following simple terms: if an equity annually brings in revenue R, and the interest rate is i, the equity is worth $K = R/i$, since R/i loaned at this rate would thus bring in R per year. See Alain Lipietz, *Le monde enchanté*, Paris: La Découverte-Maspero, 1983, p. 107.

of money-capital as a stake in future economic and political processes (we will return to this point in Chapter 5).

Marx identifies three forms of fictitious capital: credit money, government bonds and shares. On this point as with others – think, for example, of the *Manifesto*'s prophetic pages on globalisation – Marx displayed staggering capacities of foresight. For while credit money and financial markets occupied only a limited place in his era, today they are at the very heart of the functioning of economies.

Credit money may seem the form most difficult to identify as a species of fictitious capital. Is it not interest-bearing capital, rather than fictitious capital? A matter of idle funds whose owners want to lend them in exchange for interest? The correct answer is that credit money shares characteristics with both these types of finance capital.[24] It begins with a bank loan, which, having been a simple monetary sign, becomes money through circulation. But this circulation itself largely results from an *ex nihilo* creation, in that it is an advance on a future revenue and essentially does not come from previously saved funds. The generalisation of credit money since the mid-twentieth century implies 'the a-priori canonisation of private labour as social labour'.[25] Firms' production and the labour of worker-borrowers is pre-validated by money before commodities are actually sold or wages actually paid. The generalisation of this type of credit, which has long sustained economic growth, is made possible by a certain regularity of economic activities. Indeed, deposits rely on the promise that it will be possible to withdraw them in the form of notes issued by the central bank; yet no bank is able to keep to this promise if a large number of depositors want to withdraw their money simultaneously (a bank run). After all, except for reserve funds, all deposits are nothing but numbers, without any immediately available counterpart. If there is a lack of confidence in a particular bank, and even more so when there is a lack of confidence in the banking system in general, only the central bank – which has the supreme monetary power of issuing the money that serves as the banks' reserve fund – is able to prevent or contain the

24 Guttmann, 'Les mutations du capital financier', p. 77.
25 Lipietz, *Le monde enchanté*, p. 140.

financial panic. This evidences both the hierarchical nature of money as an institution and the political regulation associated with fictitious capital.[26] Credit money's fictitious dimension and its political anchoring are both accentuated by the fact that the government bonds that commercial banks sell to central banks under repurchase agreements constitute a sizeable part of the raw materials serving private banks' creation of credit money. In 2010–12, the banking/public-debt-crisis spiral in the countries of the European periphery forcefully illustrated the destructive power of such an imbrication. Here, the important question was the European Central Bank's refusal to commit to any unconditional automatic repurchase of the various countries' public debts. This not only cut off the peripheral countries' access to financial markets but simultaneously led to a rapid devalorisation of government bonds. This in turn massively weakened the banks who held large volumes of these titles. The lack of any such guarantee brutally demonstrated the single currency's fundamental policy shortfalls. Politics is credit money's guarantor of last resort. It alone can allow the controlled expansion of credit money and prevent it from abruptly contracting in turbulent periods.

The fictitious character of public debt is more immediately apparent. Indeed, it does not have any counterpart in capital valorised through production processes. Even if the expenses financed by debt do relate to investment in infrastructure or the education system, they have no direct monetary return to which the repayments correspond. Certainly, the state holds financial assets (debts, shares) and a physical estate, but essentially the latter is not supposed to be ceded. Ultimately, even though the financial management of state assets is becoming increasingly important in the current context – in particular through the selling off of the family jewels in the context of austerity plans – it is claims on the amount of future taxation that dominate public debt. Moreover, the principal on the debt is never repaid, because new issuing is constantly used to compensate the payment of securities reaching maturity. The fact that government bonds are tradeable

---

26   For an introduction to contemporary monetary mechanisms, enriched with descriptive elements focusing on France, see Dominique Plihon and Esther Jeffers, 'Le shadow banking system et la crise financière', *Les cahiers français*, 375 (2013).

further perfects their fetish character. For the individual bondholder, the fiction becomes a reality when he finds a buyer for his bonds. But these bonds do not in themselves have any direct counterpart in the valorisation process: they are advances on tax receipts.

This singular characteristic of liquidity, mentioned at the beginning of the chapter, is just as essential to market-listed stocks and corporate bonds exchanged on the financial markets. Unlike public debt, these latter do indeed represent a real capital – that is, capital invested by firms or used in their operations. Here, it is the duplication implicit in the financial mode of valorisation that is at the origin of the fiction:

> But the capital does not exist twice over, once as the capital-value of ownership titles, the shares, and then again as the actual capital invested or to be invested in the enterprises in question. It exists only in the latter form, and the share is nothing but an ownership title, *pro rata*, to the surplus-value which this capital is to realize.[27]

The same is true of company bonds, albeit with the difference that here it is a matter of credits and not property titles, and the capitalised revenues are thus interest, not dividends or really accumulated capital.

Table 1 offers a simple presentation of the basic forms of fictitious capital. It underlines the various bases of this fiction and the different modalities through which it is constituted as an economic object. In the case of bank credit, and more precisely the credit issued by banks beyond their reserve funds, the fiction rests on the fact that no revenue has been received in advance and on the anticipation of a future accumulation process. Nonetheless, this fiction is regulated in so far as the foreseen repayments are meant to be compatible with what is considered the normal development of business. With traditional bank credit, the banks hold onto the debts so they are not subject to a re-evaluation process.[28] This broad category of bank credit also includes commercial

---

27   Marx, *Capital*, Vol. III, p. 597.
28   Of course this is no longer the case today, with a large part of debts securitised in order to allow their circulation.

Table 1: Basic categories of fictitious capital in Marx

	Expression of revenues resulting from realised accumulation	Investment in future accumulation processes	Tradable on the basis of capitalised revenues
Bank credit	No, except for the part corresponding to savings-deposits	Yes	No
Public debt	Yes	No	Interest flows
Company bonds	Yes	Yes	Interest flows
Shares	Yes, but also from speculation	Yes	Dividend flows and ownership over the productive capital that firms will accumulate

credits that banks acquire from companies in transactions discounting inter-company debts.

In the case of public debt, the fiction derives from the fact that bonds do not correspond to any real capital accumulation process, but simply to advances on future tax receipts – receipts that themselves depend on the revenues that economic agents will draw from future economic activity. However, the tradability of these debt titles, like the tradability of shares and bonds, introduces a new dimension that gives fictitious capital its full power: its liquidity. A tradable equity simultaneously represents both access to earnings flows and a wealth that can at any instant be converted into real money at prices corresponding to the financial community's self-referential estimation of expected future returns.

The fictitious character of capital in the form of tradable equities brings us back to the paradox of liquidity. While banking crises correspond to a lack of *a posteriori* validation of credit money and manifest themselves in bank runs, financial crises translate into the stock-market collapses that occur when too many agents try to offload their securities simultaneously.

In sum, fictitious capital is an incarnation of that capital which tends to free itself from the process of valorisation-through-production. According to the Marxist approach, capital is fictitious to the extent that it circulates without production yet having been realised, representing a claim on a future real valorisation process. Today this fictitious capital can rely on public authorities' support, in particular the support of central banks. As they take action in favour of financial stability, these latter effect a social pre-validation of the accumulation process by way of fictitious capital. As Marx understood, fictitious capital plays a profoundly ambivalent role. On the one hand, it is a factor favouring capitalist development, to the extent that this anticipation operation allows the acceleration of the rhythm of capital accumulation. Here, we have the spirit of the nineteenth-century 'banking school', for whom the creation of money should respond to agents' needs, as well as the spirit of the Keynesian approach, which considers that the full employment of economic resources does not happen all by itself. On the other hand, fictitious capital's anticipation of future accumulation implies a radical form of fetishism liable to mutate into unsustainable phantasmagoria. The mass of accumulated fictitious capital can, then, assume proportions incompatible with the real production potential of economies. This reasoning is closer to that of the first theorists of fictitious capital, and indeed to Hayek. If this is indeed the case, then the over-accumulation of fictitious capital will inexorably lead to crisis.

CHAPTER FOUR

The Contemporary Rise of Fictitious Capital

Thomas Piketty's cult book *Capital in the Twenty-First Century* strikingly documents the explosion of inequalities of income – and even more so, of wealth – since the 1980s. This is a work of massive political consequence. It shows that meritocracy is just a myth in contemporary capitalist economies and that there is no basis for the idea that cutting taxes for the richest will have indirect repercussions that favour the poorest (the trickledown effect). Piketty has issued a huge challenge to the hegemony of conservative thought. In this sense, James Pethokoukis of the American Enterprise Institute was not mistaken in saying that 'The soft Marxism in *Capital*, if unchallenged, will spread … reshap[ing] the political economic landscape on which all future policy battles will be waged.'[1] However, despite its merits, Piketty's book poses numerous theoretical problems, which have been widely discussed since its publication. The problem that particularly interests us here concerns the ambiguities in Piketty's conception of capital and, more precisely, the gap between the theoretical definition the book mobilises and the one used in the statistics underpinning its demonstration.[2]

Piketty's theoretical analysis establishes that capital's share of overall income (α) equals the profit rate (r) multiplied by the ratio between the stock of capital (K) and production (Y): $\alpha = r(K/Y)$. This ratio is associated with a definition of capital as a factor of production – that is, the machines, buildings, software, etc., used in production. Conversely, in his empirical analysis Piketty considers the relation $\alpha = r. \beta$, according to which capital's share of overall income (α) equals capital returns (r) multiplied by the ratio of capital-wealth to

---

1   James Pethokoukis, 'The New Marxism', *The National Review*, 24 March 2014.

2   Robert Rowthorn, 'A note on Piketty's *Capital in the Twenty-first Century*', Centre for Business Research, University of Cambridge Working Paper No. 462, 2014.

revenue (β). He thus slides from an analytical notion of capital as a factor of production to an empirical definition of capital-wealth that includes shares, bonds, credits, intellectual property titles, the mass of real-estate assets, etc. This inconsistency between his theoretical and empirical categorisation of capital has major consequences for how we interpret the recent period.

Effectively, Piketty associates the rise in income inequalities with the rise in the wealth to income ratio (β), while also proposing explanations that concern capital's weight in production, as a factor of production (K/Y). For him, the reason why capital's share of income increases as the capital intensity (K/Y) of production grows is that contemporary economies allow multiple uses of capital (K). In this perspective, the deepening of income inequalities originates from structural transformations at the level of production and is aggravated by socio-political power relations turning in capital's favour.

This explanation firstly poses a problem on the conceptual terrain, since the rate of exploitation (α – the share of revenue captured by capital) here appears as a result and not as a determinant of the profit rate. It thus contributes to the mystification according to which capital has an autonomous capacity to create value. Most importantly, however, it is unconvincing on the empirical terrain. For several decades we have seen an investment slowdown in the developed economies (see Chapter 6), as expressed by the stabilisation or fall in the capital intensity in production.[3] Conversely, as Piketty shows, there has been a considerable rise in the wealth to income ratio (β). To explain the rise of capital's share of income ($\nearrow\alpha$), it is thus necessary to think through the disconnection between the evolution of the wealth to income ratio (β) and capital intensity in production (K/Y). And it is precisely the rise of fictitious capital that allows us to think through how sluggish investment in production can go hand-in-hand with the vast expansion of wealth and wealth inequalities.

---

3   As shown by Piketty's figures concerning the stock of capital without capital gains and corporate capital-output ratios (at book value). See Thomas Piketty and Gabriel Zucman, 'Capital is back: wealth-income ratios in rich countries 1700–2010', Appendix, Figures A133 and A71, piketty.pse.ens.fr, July 2013.

Now that we have given the concept of fictitious capital a solid theoretical anchoring, we can describe the evolution of its empirical forms and thus bring to light a dimension largely underplayed in Piketty's work. This chapter will show that, in the rich world as a whole, the various categories of fictitious capital have developed at irregular rhythms, though they are often synchronised across the various different countries. This allows us to document a process essential to understanding capitalism's contemporary conjuncture, namely the rise of the volume of payment commitments anticipating future production relative to the wealth that is actually produced. Seen from this angle, financialisation appears as a systemic flight of fancy that the great crisis of 2007–8 was not enough to halt.

We will begin with a more specific description of the categories of fictitious capital identified by Marx, namely private sector credit, public debt and stock-market capitalisation. These were presented in Table 1. We will then turn to other forms of fictitious capital whose contours are harder to make out – forms resulting from the rising sophistication of contemporary finance systems.

The basic forms of fictitious capital

To simplify our explanation somewhat, our study of the dynamic of fictitious capital's basic forms in the main high-income countries will concentrate on the five most important rich economies (US, Japan, Germany, France, UK). In order to underline that this is indeed a tendency common across high-income countries, I will also give the average (mean) figures for the eleven richest countries.[4]

The first indicator we will use is the total credits to the non-financial private sector in each of the domestic economies concerned. This includes banking credit and the whole array of other forms of credit (inter-company commercial credits, bonds) accorded to non-financial enterprises, non-profit institutions and households – international credits included. Focusing on the non-financial private sector allows us to leave the developments endogenous to the financial sphere to

---

4   The other six countries are Canada, Italy, the Netherlands, South Korea, Australia and Spain.

one side for the moment. We will instead fix our sights on the commitments made by agents directly involved in the productive sector and their capacity to generate wealth. Indeed, we would not necessarily be unwarranted in considering credit as a whole to be fictitious capital, to the extent that – with the suspension of the Bretton Woods system – the whole monetary system now rests on bank money. Unlike in the gold-standard system, money has no anchoring other than its social acceptability, guaranteed by the state and regulated by central bank policies. In such a system, money – which principally circulates between the bank accounts of economic agents – comes from loans accorded by banks. This is the principle whereby credits make up deposits. Finally, in examining the credit supplied to both companies and households, we can understand the speculation processes taking place in the real-estate sector.

Figure 8 shows that the spectacular boom in credit to the non-financial private sector has been a general phenomenon since the 1970s. If at that time it amounted to 72 per cent of the average GDP, this figure had risen to 174 per cent by 2007. The only country where this tendency was reversed in the 1990s was Japan. In those years the country underwent a major financial crisis, representing the backlash after a speculation bubble provoked by the 1985 Plaza Accord's decision to

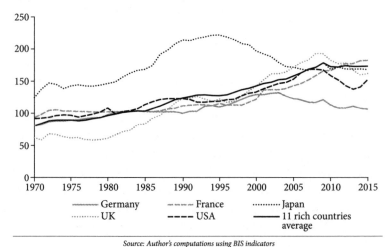

Source: Author's computations using BIS indicators

Figure 8: Credit to the non-financial private sector (per cent of GDP)

re-evaluate the Yen. Since 2003, this tendency has also dropped off in Germany. Another important consideration here is the fact that the financial crisis led to a sharp and simultaneous halt of credit in all countries in 2009, attesting to the truly global character of the credit crunch. It is also worth noting that, while in the 2000s there was a generalised acceleration of credit (with the exception of Japan), it took on particularly vast proportions in the US and UK. In the aftermath of the financial crisis, the weight of private debt tended to stabilise in most countries as firms and households deleveraged. Note that France is an exception in this regard, with a ratio of private debt to GDP now surpassing that of all the other countries under consideration.

Figure 9 represents the evolution of the second type of fictitious capital mentioned by Marx: public debt. Over the first decades of the postwar period, sustained growth and inflation allowed the erosion of the very high debt levels inherited from the Second World War. But this tendency was overturned from the 1970s onward. The mean debt-to-GDP ratio in the eleven countries can be broken down into three periods. From the mid-1970s to the mid-1990s there was a rise in public indebtedness, on average rising from around 30 to 65 per cent of GDP. This development was linked to the generalisation of public deficits, but was strongly amplified from the 1980s onward by raised

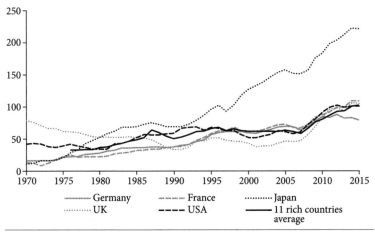

Source: Author's computations using BIS, Reinhardt and Rogoff, AMECO and OECD Indicators

Figure 9: Credit to the government sector (per cent of GDP)

real interest rates, which generated a snowball effect automatically increasing the weight of the debt. From 1995 to 2008, this ratio stabilised, before abruptly rising again from 2008 onward in reaction to the financial crisis, hitting 100 per cent in 2015. This general pattern masks significant discrepancies. The stabilisation of 1995–2007 was uneven. We can see various diverging patterns in this period: a notable decrease in Canada, Australia, Spain and the Netherlands; relative stability in the UK, France, the US and Italy; and a significant rise in Germany and South Korea. The most spectacular case was Japan, which saw an explosion in its public debt as it worked to deal with the consequences of its financial crisis in a context of prolonged stagnation. Passing from 69 per cent of GDP in 1991 to 155 per cent in 2005, it hit more than 220 per cent in the years following the 2008 crisis.

Figure 10 concerns a third type of fictitious capital: the stock-market capitalisation of listed domestic companies, whose value reflects the market valorisation of anticipated profits. The graph presents the pattern of stock-market capitalisation relative to GDP since 1975 for the main rich economies and since 1979 for our eleven-country average. Japan once again shows an atypical trajectory. After hitting a record level of 130 per cent in 1989, this ratio plunged to 53 per cent in 2002, after the bursting of the dotcom bubble. Conversely, the respective

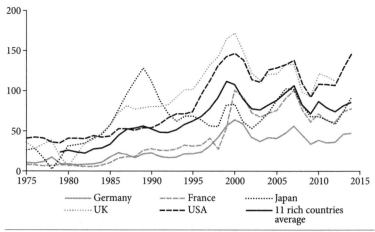

Source: Author's computations using World Bank Global Financial Development Indicators

Figure 10: Stock market capitalisation (per cent of GDP)

profiles of the other countries are relatively similar. The 1980s and 1990s saw a two-stage rise in the ratio, which reached its maximum in 2001, before falling in two further stages following the 2001 crunch and the crisis of 2008–9. Despite this partial reflux, the long-term rise is considerable. The mean ratio passed from 24 per cent in 1979 to 85 per cent in 2015, peaking at 111 per cent in 1999. This development was most impressive in the US and the UK, rising from 40 per cent and 35 per cent respectively in 1975 to 146 per cent for the US in 2014 and 112 per cent for the UK in 2012, after having peaked at 146 per cent and 171 per cent respectively in 2001. There was the same tendency in Germany, albeit at a much lower level: having stood at 10 per cent of GDP in 1975, stock-market capitalisation reached a level of 64 per cent by the millennium, before settling down at 47 per cent in 2014.

Crucially, the contemporary accumulation of fictitious capital on the stock markets is closely connected to the addiction to fossil fuels. Current market trends show capital's projections for a future still based on carbon. Indeed, the hydrocarbon reserves claimed by the major oil companies very largely determine their valorisation, because they constitute the basis for forecasting future profits. However, according to IPCC estimates, if we are to keep the temperature rise beneath the 2°C limit, then we will have to leave somewhere between two-thirds and four-fifths of these reserves unused. Companies in the energy sector, together with those in the directly affected industrial sectors, represent close to one-third of worldwide stock-market capitalisation. Taking the political measures necessary to halt fossil fuel extraction would immediately result in a knock-on destabilisation of the financial markets. Bank of England governor Mark Carney warned as much in autumn 2015, when he evoked the 'tragedy of the horizon'. He was referring to a 'tragedy' resulting from the fact that the likely effects of these changes lie beyond decision-makers' own temporal horizons:

> A wholesale reassessment of prospects, especially if it were to occur suddenly, could potentially destabilise markets, spark a pro-cyclical crystallisation of losses and a persistent tightening of financial

conditions. In other words, an abrupt resolution of the tragedy of horizons is in itself a financial stability risk.[5]

Here, the preservation of fictitious capital on the stock market directly impedes the fight against global warming.

Figure 11 adds together the weight of the different types of fictitious capital relative to GDP in each of the main countries for which stock-market data is available over a sufficiently long period. It is very noticeable that the heterogeneity among different areas is tending to fall in this regard. While this ratio reached a first peak of 407 per cent of GDP in Japan at the height of the extreme speculation episode of the late 1980s, even this was surpassed in 2005 (415 per cent), progressively growing to a maximum of 485 per cent in 2014. While in Germany its expansion was interrupted in the 2000s, for all the other countries it grew at a near-regular rate across this period. The average (mean) rose almost continually, multiplying by a factor of 2.5 in just over three decades: from 151 per cent of GDP in 1979 to 358 per cent in 2014. Although each financial crisis (1989, 2001, 2008) brought a reduction in the weight of fictitious capital, on each occasion it quickly resumed its upward trend.

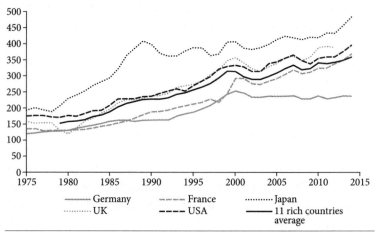

Source: Author's computations using figures 8, 9 and 10 data

Figure 11: Total weight of the basic forms of fictitious capital (per cent of GDP)

5   Mark Carney, 'Breaking the tragedy of the horizon – climate change and financial stability', speech given at Lloyd's of London, 29 September 2015.

In short, the different basic forms of fictitious capital combined to ensure that, overall, this category expanded across the whole period in question, including after the 2008 crisis. In other words, over the last three decades, the quantity of value validated in anticipation of future valorisation processes has constantly increased relative to the quantity of wealth actually produced.

THE SOPHISTICATED FORMS OF FICTITIOUS CAPITAL

The boom in the elementary forms of fictitious capital is based on an accumulation dynamic in which factors like the liberalisation of credit, the adoption of a new anti-inflationary monetary policy, and the flow of capitals toward the countries of the North played a crucial role.[6] Since the early 1980s, even the temporary dips owing to financial crises have not reversed this tendency, with public debt taking up the slack from the contraction of credit and the fall in equity prices. At a more qualitative level, this expansion of fictitious capital has led it to go beyond its elementary forms. The development and sophistication of what were previously instruments of only marginal importance is truly transforming finance.[7] The first decisive point is the decline of bank intermediation in favour of market finance – that is, the issuing of shares and bonds on finance markets. This development, which first affected finance in the Anglo-Saxon world, is little by little spreading – albeit at unequal rhythms – across all rich countries. This has been encouraged by information and communications technology, which has contributed to breaking the banks' monopoly by making data on companies and stock quotations much more accessible as well as improving financial markets' efficiency in terms of both speed and volume.

Borrowers have adopted equity finance because it allows them to obtain lower interest rates. It also implies a formalisation of the

---

6   Greta R. Krippner, *Capitalizing on Crisis: The Political Origins of the Rise of Finance*, Cambridge, MA: Harvard University Press, 2011.

7   Robert Guttmann has provided a perfect description of this process in 'Les mutations du capital financier' and 'A primer on finance-led capitalism and its crisis', *Revue de la Régulation*, No. 3/4 (2008), regulation.revues.org.

information they have to publish in order to obtain funds, thus allowing them to escape a relation with bankers that is often perceived as overly intrusive. As for capital suppliers, the superiority of market finance owes to the fact that in normal periods they can liquidate their positions at any moment. This liquidity offers increased flexibility in managing savings, which is crucial for collective funds and pension funds but also for insurance companies, whose liabilities have grown strongly in recent decades.

The second essential dimension is the liberalisation of exchange rates that took place in the 1970s with the break-up of the Bretton Woods monetary system. Indeed, currency fluctuations offer opportunities for speculation and, for non-financial agents, a need for increased coverage. Flexible exchange rates and market finance have allowed an explosion of new sectors of fictitious capital standing one degree further from production processes than the basic forms. Contract swaps, structured products and option contracts are multiplying and combining among themselves. They are limited by nothing other than the imaginations of financial actors themselves. The latter's creativity is, indeed, highly animated, but is limited to redefining the type of contractual arrangement linking the funds provider to the borrower. As such, the frenetic financial innovations of the 1980s, 1990s and 2000s were never anything more than a multiplication of the means of organising chains of indebtedness. These new forms of fictitious capital have essentially flourished in an unregulated grey zone separate from the official finance markets – so-called 'shadow banking'.

Authors working on contemporary finance often – and quite rightly – emphasise the process of banking disintermediation. This is where borrowers increasingly meet their financing needs on the finance markets rather than through banks. The paradox is that the decline in the banks' intermediation role has ultimately led to a multiplication of the intermediaries standing between borrowers and savers. Indeed, this fragmented intermediation is characteristic of shadow banking.

The banks' traditional intermediation role consists of establishing relations among savers/depositors. It involves the combination of two distinct operations, the first of which consists of a qualitative transformation of credits. While there is a relatively significant risk that the households or companies to whom banks lend will default, the banks themselves are more solid, and the credits that private individuals accord to them through their savings and current accounts are far more secure. This is all the more true given the existence of explicit and implicit forms of state support for the banking system, in particular given their privileged access to the money issued by the central bank as well as deposit-guarantee mechanisms. The second operation allows the transformation of maturities, meaning the exchange of – typically short-term – deposits for long-term borrowing. This two-pronged intermediation operation allows savers to benefit from economies of scale linked to the diversification and mutualisation of risk and of supervisory efforts.

With the liberalisation of finance, the banks face competition from new actors like mutual funds or monetary funds in providing this intermediation role. Reacting to this threat and seeking to profit from the new opportunities, they try to get around regulation on compulsory reserves, thus allowing them to economise on their own funds. The transfer of part of their assets into Special Purpose Vehicles feeds the development of a new type of banking system.

Shadow banking is a parallel credit system that breaks the intermediation function down into multiple stages.[8] As Robert Guttmann stresses, it differs from both finance intermediated by a regulated banking system and the market finance whose transactions are public: it is *network finance*, i.e. a specific form of finance constituted of a multitude of opaque and interdependent bilateral transactions.[9] It tends to transform finance into what we could call a *multi-intermediation*. The link between the ultimate borrower and the initial lender is distended. Financial gains are captured across the whole length of the chain, in the form of commissions and charges. Starting from the borrowers' end of things, the main links in the chain are: 1) the distribution of loans to households or firms or the issuance of derivatives products; 2) their packaging; 3) the creation of asset-backed securities on the basis

---

8   Zoltan Poszar, Tobias Adrian, Adam Ashcraft and Hayley Boesky, 'Shadow banking', *Economic Policy Review*, 19:2 (2013), newyorkfed.org.

9   Robert Guttmann, *Financial-led Capitalism: Shadow Banking, Re-Regulation, and the Future of Global Markets*, New York: Palgrave Macmillan, 2015.

of these packages of financial products; 4) the combination of these packages of securities, including options contracts, in order to form a sort of financial *mille-feuille*: Collateralised Debt Obligations; and 5) their sale to investors on the financial markets.

The set of institutions that underpin these chains' functioning are connected to the rest of the economy by monetary funds and repo markets. The former resemble a kind of quasi-money. They offer to remunerate households and firms – but also public bodies – in the form of what are normally very liquid investments in real-estate credit and commercial paper (short-term credit to companies). Repo markets are also short-term loan markets. They are securitised, as the borrower provides the lender with equity as collateral, equivalent to the loaned money plus a calculation of risk.[10] These money markets were the principal channel through which the crisis spread in 2007–8: when they suddenly dried up, this blocked households' and companies' access to credit, as well as inter-bank credit.

In summary, shadow-banking operations add a transformation of liquidity to the traditional operations transforming maturities and transforming the quality of credits. Typically, this means packaging the isolated credits accorded to individuals and firms, which can only be passed on at low prices in order to make them into securities that can be sold more expensively thanks to the combination of different types of risk (different maturities, different types of borrowers) – and, of course, the quality certification offered by ratings agencies…

This break with the classic banking system's regulatory framework has undoubtedly given fresh dynamism to US banking. Yet it has been accompanied by greater opacity as well as a loss of risk measurement regarding the relations established between borrowers and savers. Ultimately, this resulted in the disaster we are now all aware of. On the other side of the Atlantic, the traditional big European banks have played a crucial role in the internationalisation of shadow banking.[11] On the one hand, they have connected to the US parallel banking circuit through active borrowing on the money markets and the en masse buying of the derivatives and structured credits issued by US

---

10 Ragot, 'Les banques centrales dans la tempête', pp. 389, 393.

11 Plihon and Jeffers, 'Le shadow banking system et la crise financière'.

institutions. On the other hand, they have created and developed their own parallel intermediation system through collective investment funds (UCITS) and alternative funds. These latter mobilise savers' deposits and the banks' access to ECB refinancing in service of aggressive speculation strategies.

More generally, commercial banks that were initially threatened by the relative decline in banking credit are increasingly engaged in securities markets and have massively invested in the parallel banking system. Their operations on their own account make markets more liquid and thus safer. Moreover, their supply of funds facilitates the buying of securities through indebtedness (the leverage effect). Finally, through pyramiding they accept securities as guarantees for loans, with a view to acquiring further securities, thus allowing them to realise sizeable transactions with very little initial capital. In a logic resembling the one described by Minsky, this has the effect of creating a self-sustaining demand for financial products, since the rise in asset prices increases the available collateral and thus frees up loans for buying new securities.

In this new context, marked by the development of derivative products and shadow banking, speculation is no longer limited to boom periods. Instead it becomes an activity independent of the cyclical process, in particular thanks to derivative products' great flexibility. Here, we have an extremely dynamic incarnation of fictitious capital. Nonetheless, it is rather difficult to capture this explosion in the sophisticated forms of fictitious capital in empirical terms, firstly because we do not have extensive enough data series and secondly because the different categories overlap. However, the figures on the evolution of the exchange market, derivatives transactions and the size of the parallel banking system do indeed indicate a rapid growth in the sophisticated forms of fictitious capital over the course of the recent period.

Daily transaction levels on the exchange markets have increased considerably in the last quarter-century. In order to provide an evaluation of the fictitious dimension of these transactions, we have to compare them to the size of the trade flows in commodities and FDI. This is what Figure 12 allows us to do. Between 1989 and 2013, the sums exchanged on the exchange markets each day rose from $620bn to

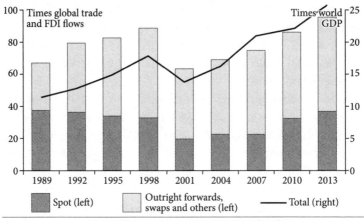

Source: Author's computations using BIS, UNCTAD and IMF data

Figure 12: Daily foreign exchange transactions

$5,344bn. It is striking to note the discrepancy between transactions corresponding to commercial or investment operations and those corresponding to a purely financial register: the latter represented seventy times more than the former at the beginning of this period, and 100 times more by its end. This development, itself following a rapid advance over the course of the 1980s,[12] took place in two stages: strong growth in the 1990s, wiped away at the turn of the 2000s by the dual shock of the financial crises in the emerging economies (including the Asian, Russian, Turkish and Argentinian crises) and the bursting of the dotcom bubble; and then an even stronger recovery in the course of the 2000s, but this time seemingly not interrupted by the crisis emanating from US subprime real-estate credit. The other striking element is the relative decline in the share of spot transactions, which passed from 56 per cent in 1989 to 30 per cent in 2007, in favour of derivatives contracts. We might remember that these products did not even exist until 1972, with the victory in the battle to create a currency futures market as part of the Chicago Mercantile Exchange.

The figures for derivatives as a whole – thus including exchange derivatives – are even more fragmentary. The Bank for International

---

12   François Chesnais, *La mondialisation du capital*, Paris: Syros, 1997.

Settlements data series only begins in 1993 for organised markets and 1998 for over-the-counter markets – that is, for the transactions conducted outside of any regulatory framework. Nonetheless, even the trend over this limited period is staggering. These contracts corresponded to sums representing three times world GDP in 1998 and more than ten times by 2007, before falling back to 6.7 times in 2015 (Figure 13). This amount should be understood in relative terms, in that it concerns a notional value – that is, the value of the securities on which basis the different derivatives contracts are established. Nonetheless, the sums actually engaged are considerable – they peaked at 55 per cent of GDP in 2008, before falling to 20 per cent by 2015.

Another fact worth noting is that these derivatives prospered above all in the context of over-the-counter transactions – that is, transactions free of any form of regulation. This is what allowed cumulative leverage effects reaching up to a factor of fifty: an initial capital of just 20,000 euros allows for a 1 million dollar investment, with the rest being borrowed. When everything goes well, this generates outstanding returns. Conversely, a drop of just 2 per cent eliminates the entire underlying capital and leads to a collapse along the whole chain of transactions.[13]

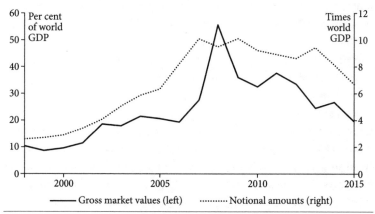

Source: Author's computations using BIS and IMF data

Figure 13: Total outstanding amount of over-the-counter derivatives contracts

13   Gillian Tett, 'The unease bubbling in today's brave new financial world', FT.com, 19 January 2007.

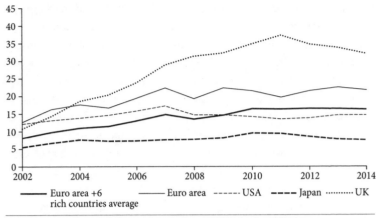

Source: Author's computations using Financial Stability Board and OECD data

Figure 14: Assets of non-bank, non-insurance, non-pension fund,
non-public financial intermediaries (per cent of GDP)

The explosion of second-generation fictitious capital is also apparent in the very rapid growth of the parallel banking system in the
United States since the 1980s. While, at that time, its supply of credit
represented only a fraction of banking credit, it became more important from the mid-1990s onward, reaching close to $17tn (some 120
per cent of US GDP) by 2007.[14] Recently, the Financial Stability Board's
annual report on shadow banking provided a basis for an international
comparison of the weight of non-bank, non-insurance, non-pension
fund, non-public financial intermediaries (Figure 14). The rise of this
sector has been particularly spectacular in the UK, increasing from
11 per cent of GDP in 2002 to 42 per cent in 2011. Elsewhere, the rise
was less impressive but still very significant, typically meaning a doubling of these financial institutions' weight during the first decade of
the century and a moderate decline – although it was very significant
in the US – in the aftermath of the financial crisis. Another lesson is
that the UK is by far the most exposed country in terms of the size of
shadow banking relative to GDP, followed by the Eurozone.

The concept of fictitious capital deployed by Hayek and Marx is
valuable in that it directly poses the problematic relationship between

---

14 Poszar et al., 'Shadow banking'.

real accumulation and financial accumulation. While for Hayek fictitious capital upsets resource allocation and leads to wastage, Marx takes a subtler view. For him, the anticipated validation of the valorisation process can, up to a certain point, stimulate the real accumulation process. Nonetheless, he clearly emphasises the disruptive effects that can result from financial phantasmagoria. Moreover, his conception of fictitious capital extends beyond the particular question of banking credit, which monopolises the Austrian school's attention. Marx's analytical framework is thus both richer and more nuanced. Thanks to his typology, we have been able to describe booms in the different forms of fictitious capital over recent decades.

The explosion of fictitious capital reveals a dizzying growth in the quantity of value validated in anticipation of the accumulation process linked to commodity production. Appearing in the context of the deregulation of financial activities and flexible exchange rates, this dynamic results from a widening of the traditional channels of indebtedness and stock-market valorisation. It has now doubled, with a second-generation finance operating as a derivation of the first type of fictitious capital. Over the last three decades, this phenomenon has spread across all the big economies. However, Germany and Japan have distinguished themselves from other countries. The rise in the weight of the basic forms of fictitious capital in Germany was interrupted in the early 2000s, while in Japan the 1990 financial crisis led to a decade-long shrinkage of fictitious capital. This fall has now more than been cancelled out.

Without doubt, when we study the basic forms of fictitious capital, the main lesson is that its various incarnations – credit, stock-market valorisation and public debt – have combined to produce a regular expansion of fictitious capital across the period concerned. We should emphasise that, at this aggregate level, the 2008 crisis did not mark a turnaround. Rather, it put an end to the extremely rapid expansion of certain sophisticated forms of fictitious capital over the last two decades – namely, derivative products and shadow banking. The exception was currency exchange operations, whose rise continued.

CHAPTER FIVE

Financial Accumulation

In her widely discussed book *Capitalizing on Crisis*, Greta Krippner defines financialisation as a reorientation of capital accumulation away from productive and commercial activities toward ones concerning finance. In the 1970s and 1980s, the deregulation of financial markets, the rise in interest rates and the influx of international capitals resulted in economic reorganisation, with the search for profits now increasingly passing through financial channels. Empirically documenting this phenomenon in the United States up to the 2001 crisis, her book is doubly valuable. Firstly, because it places the motor of capitalism – that is, profits – at the centre of financialisation; secondly, because it allows us to appreciate the full extent of a process that is often referenced but rarely grasped in its totality, and indeed to pin down its contours.

This chapter will adopt the same approach, in order to demonstrate that the turn toward financial accumulation is not limited to the United States. I will not be offering such a systematic panorama as Krippner's, not least given that data for the main rich economies equivalent to the figures she uses are either hard to access or incomplete. Nonetheless, empirical considerations will allow us to give an account of a marked tendency that these economies all have in common, even if it takes a different form and intensity in each country.

We can mobilise three types of indicators to prove that economies are being financialised: the weight of the financial sector, the importance of this sector's profits relative to overall profits, and the dynamic of financial profits in non-financial firms.

THE WEIGHT OF THE FINANCIAL SECTOR

We can see a continual increase in the weight of financial activities dating back to the 1980s. Figure 15 sets out from a broad definition of finance, including all financial-mediation, insurance and real-estate activities. It shows that in the main rich countries the added value

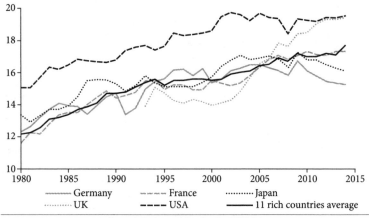

Source: Author's computations based on OECD data

Figure 15: Gross value added of financial insurance
and real-estate activities (per cent of GDP)

recorded in this sector has constantly increased as a proportion of
GDP, with an average 50 per cent rise over this period. The extent of
this development suggests that, aside from the increased importance
of the service sector, the characteristic structural mutation in the big
developed economies is financialisation – a process coming to a halt in
countries like the US and France since the financial crisis and receding
in Japan and Germany.

Figure 16 presents the added value in financial and insurance activities alone. However, despite a broadly similar trend, we find more
contrasted national trajectories. The upward trend is particularly
important in the US and the UK up to the late 2000s, but there has
been no general increase in the weight of these activities in the French,
German and Japanese economies since the 1990s – indeed, in France
they have retreated.

Figure 17 shows the profits from financial and insurance activities
as a share of overall profits. These calculations are based on gross profits
(gross operating profits) for reasons regarding both the availability
of statistics and the concern to avoid problems linked to calculating
amortisation. It shows that, on average, from 1980 up to the crisis, this
share increased constantly. In the US, most of the rise occurred during

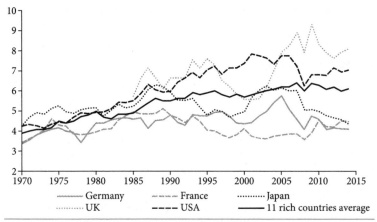

Source: Author's computations based on OECD data

Figure 16: Gross value added by financial and
insurance activities (per cent of GDP)

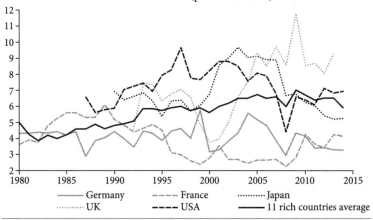

Source: Author's computations based on OECD data

Figure 17: Financial and insurance activities gross operating
surplus (per cent of total gross operating surplus)

the late 1980s and 1990s. In the UK and Japan, the dynamics were less
even, with a surge in the 2000s.

In France, conversely, the growth of the 1980s rapidly came to
an end. Thus began a slow decline lasting until the 2008 crisis. We
might note that the sector's share of overall profits rebounded in the

post-crisis context thanks to the effectiveness of the government rescue measures from which it benefited, whereas the rest of the economy remained mired in stagnation. Data for Germany does not indicate any long-term trend.

Non-financial companies' financial income is the third indicator useful for giving an account of the turn toward financial accumulation. It establishes the relation between this sector's gross profits and the dividends and interest it receives. Data regarding capital gains – the profits resulting from the resale of securities at a price higher than their purchase price – are only available for the United States. Nonetheless, we might suppose that they do not have a predominant share of all firms' financial income, as in the US their share has fluctuated between 20 per cent and 30 per cent since the 1990s.[1]

The graphs show strongly contradictory developments (Figures 18a to 18e). The extreme case is France, where non-financial firms' financial income has constantly grown relative to profits since the 1970s, rising from 8 per cent of gross operating profits (GOP) to 88 per cent in 2008. This spectacular rise of financial incomes relative to GOP in France relates to the 2000s decline of non-financial corporations' profit margins. It furthermore corresponds to a taxation system which intervenes more – relative to other countries – at the operational level rather than at the level of companies' profits. Interestingly, in the aftermath of the financial crisis this share of financial income has retreated.

As for Germany and Japan, the relevant data only goes back to the 1990s. In Germany, financial income rose from around 10 per cent of gross profits in the 1990s to above 15 per cent in the late 2000s – a level slightly lower than that of the Anglo-Saxon countries, but one that nonetheless signals that significant transformations are at work here. In Japan, the weight of non-financial firms' financial income is much

---

1   See Krippner, *Capitalizing on Crisis*, p. 38, and, for the 2000s, the author's calculations based on Internal Revenue Service data: 'SOI Tax Stats – Returns of Active Corporations - Table 6', at irs.gov.

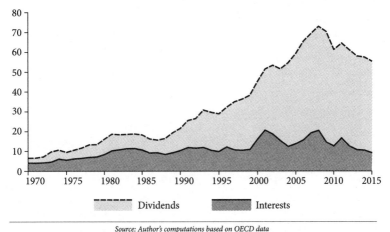

Source: Author's computations based on OECD data

Figure 18a: Non-financial corporations' financial income –
France (per cent of gross operating profit)

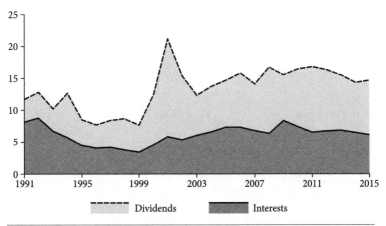

Source: Author's computations based on OECD data

Figure 18b: Non-financial corporations' financial income –
Germany (per cent of gross operating profit)

lower; the phase of decline in the 1990s was followed by a marked recovery, up until the 2008 crisis. In both cases, it is worth noting the significant increase in the weight of the dividends received.

In the UK case, the interest data show a continual but slow increase up to the start of the 1990s. Numbers on dividends – which only begin

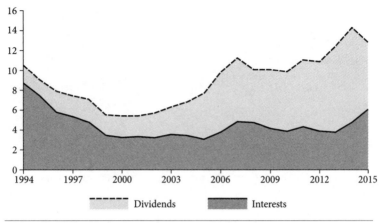

Source: Author's computations based on OECD data

Figure 18c: Non-financial corporations' financial income –
Japan (per cent of gross operating surplus)

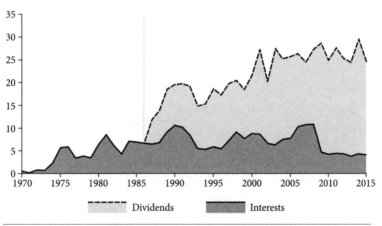

Source: Author's computations based on OECD data

Figure 18d: Non-financial corporations' financial income –
UK (per cent of gross operating surplus)

in 1987 – suggest a rapid rise in the late 1980s (from 7.2 per cent in
1987 to 14.4 per cent in 1992) and then a constant advance, more than
compensating for the decline in interest received.

The US pattern is very different. Firstly, because here interest

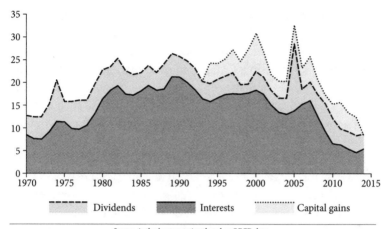

Source: Author's computations based on OECD data

Figure 18e: Non-financial corporations' financial income –
US (per cent of gross operating surplus)

makes up the greater part of firms' financial income, including the
revenues that come from investing their liquid assets in highly developed monetary funds in this country. Secondly, we might observe
that the marked rise seen in the 1970s and 1980s continued into the
1990s thanks to capital gains. This was followed by a brief decline after
the dotcom crash and a renewed surge just before the 2008 crisis,
with an average level in this period of about 25 per cent of GOP – far
higher than in the 1970s. It was only after the financial crisis that they
retreated spectacularly.

We should be cautious in drawing conclusions from these graphs,
not least given the limited possibility of comparing the datasets due to
national variations in accounting practices and taxation. Nonetheless,
what they do indicate is a general tendency for non-financial firms'
financial income to rise relative to profits. The stabilisation of this ratio
in the US from the 1990s and its limited increase in the UK should be
seen in light of the data we earlier presented regarding financial firms'
profits. Indeed, these are the two countries with the greatest increase
in the financial sector's profits as a share of all profits.

These stylised facts provide us with two main lessons. Firstly, it
seems that in the five countries under consideration the weight of the

financial sector in the wider sense (including real-estate activities) has grown in a strong and continuous fashion since the 1970s.

Secondly, they bear witness to the fact that financial profits' relative weight is increasing, giving empirical foundation to the notion of financialisation as a matter of accumulation by financial channels. There is a general tendency toward the financialisation of profits, except in Japan whose early 1990s crisis brought a halt in this regard. But the central site of its development is not the same in every context. While in France and, to a lesser extent, Germany, the main dynamic is an increase in non-financial firms' financial revenues, in the Anglo-Saxon countries it is the boom in finance sector profits that predominates. At this stage of our research, it is not easy to explain this contrast. This could be a matter of accounting trickery – for example regarding the rules according to which holdings are divided between the financial and non-financial sectors – or indeed to more structural factors, for example the relative importance of revenues associated with shares in companies operating abroad. Even so, these data solidly establish that financial methods have become increasingly important to capital accumulation.

One flaw in Krippner's work is that it does not delve into the nature of these financial profits: where do they come from? And while she does identify the causes of financialisation, she does not examine the socio-political contradictions that it entails. These questions could hardly be thornier.

CHAPTER SIX

Where Do Financial
Profits Come From?

The counterpart to the growth of fictitious capital relative to wealth produced is financial profits' increasing share of overall profits. But these financial profits are not themselves fictitious. Paid in hard cash, they have all the attributes of monetary power, first of all in terms of what is usually called purchasing power – the immediate drawing rights on wealth produced. Their only distinction from other profits is that they have no direct link with the production and exchange of commodities: they are returns generated by financial processes.

Without doubt, finance can create favourable conditions for value-production by reallocating capital from declining sectors to expanding ones. This is an essential aspect of finance – indeed, one to which we will later return. Even so, finance is never itself at the origin of value creation. Financial profits incarnate value but do not result from value production. We should thus conceive of them as transfers of income away from those activities that do produce value – that is, the revenues that come from labour and/or profits drawn from the production of goods and services. This poses no simple theoretical question, and its political stakes are of decisive importance. Identifying the economic source of financial profits is a necessary condition for giving an account of their social content and, ultimately, for thinking through their impact on capitalism's contemporary trajectory.

These are profits of a particular kind, which take different forms. The characteristic they do all have in common is their association with the circulation of money-capital.[1] These profits result from idle money being made available in exchange for remuneration. They come from the most fetishised form of capital – the form that embodies money's

---

1 Costas Lapavitsas has mounted a detailed study of the Marxist conception of financial profits (*Profiting Without Producing*, pp. 138–68). I have made use of this study in the arguments below, but I partly diverge from his approach, including in my analysis of capital gains.

magical capacity to grow without braving the risks of production, just as a pear tree produces pears. They come both from revenues that result from loan operations, share ownership and trade in financial assets, and from financial institutions' profits. Thus, we can characterise three principal types of income as financial profits: interests, dividends and the capital gains realised through the disposal of assets. These profits can enrich households – feeding the rise in inequalities – but also non-financial firms as well as financial institutions. One further type of financial profit relates to the profits that financial firms draw from their activities managing the flows of finance.[2]

THE HETEROGENEOUS SOURCES OF INTEREST

The simplest form of financial profits is that of the interest collected during loan operations. The social content of this type of income varies, from the loans given to households to those given to states or indeed to companies.

Profits upon alienation

The interest households pay corresponds to a pre-capitalist form of revenue – indeed, one whose persistence Marx himself noted. We can thank Costas Lapavitsas for having brought into relief the growing role this interest plays in contemporary economies.[3] These *profits upon alienation* correspond to a direct deduction from personal household incomes. This is a secondary form of exploitation, which takes place independent of the extraction of surplus-value in the production process. Marx distinguished between two forms of secondary

---

2   To be precise, we should also include the very high salaries and bonuses received by financial employees and indeed the employees of non-financial firms' finance departments. Indeed, these salaries have the same social content as financial profits, despite the fact that they are not formally recorded as such by national accounting bodies. Unfortunately, the available data does not allow us to explore this dimension. On this point see Olivier Godechot's 'Financialization is marketization!', and *Working Rich: Salaires, bonus et appropriation du profit dans l'industrie financière*, Paris: La Découverte, 2007.

3   Lapavitsas, *Profiting Without Producing*; Costas Lapavitsas and Irina Levina, 'Financial profit: profit from production and profit upon alienation', researchonmoneyandfinance. org, 2010.

exploitation. In the first, workers remain formally independent but their access to the means of production is conditional on the loans they are given by a particular usurer class. In the second, the interest comes from loans financing consumption. In each case, interest is a means of expropriating income from borrowers without passing via the production process. 'What takes place is exploitation by capital without the mode of production of capital.'[4]

The main rich economies have seen a powerful rise in household indebtedness since the 1970s. The amount of loans accorded to households has doubled or tripled relative to GDP in each of these countries (see the respective data in Figure 19). In Japan and Germany, this upward trend was interrupted in the early 2000s. Note the particularly high levels of household indebtedness relative to GDP in the Anglo-Saxon countries on the eve of the crisis – reaching close to 100 per cent of GDP – and the rapid contraction that followed.

Profits upon alienation grow in tandem with rising household indebtedness, whether it is used to finance housing, study, the purchase of durable goods like cars, or goods for immediate consumption. Consumer credit is one of this trend's most strikingly visible practices,

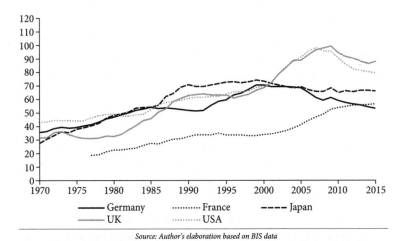

Source: Author's elaboration based on BIS data

Figure 19: Households and NPIHS debt (per cent of GDP)

---

4   Karl Marx, *Grundrisse*, Harmondsworth: Penguin, 1973, p. 853.

with specialised companies working at usurious rates; as of April 2014, the effective annual interest rate applied by the leading French consumer credit company Cofinoga stood at 19 per cent, as against the ECB refinancing rate of 0.25 per cent. Another aspect of this phenomenon is households becoming over-indebted, with their incomes no longer sufficing to honour the payments they owe to their creditors. This phenomenon has grown considerably, including because of rising unemployment. In France, the number of insolvency cases recorded by the Banque de France commission in charge of addressing this problem rose from 60,000 at the beginning of the 1990s to 150,000 in 2007, before continuing past 200,000 in 2012.

This pre-emption of labour income by finance capital is also visible at the macroeconomic level, even if the available data do not allow us to account consistently for its long-term dynamics. Three main variables explain the amount of interest that households pay relative to their available income: indebtedness, income dynamics, and interest rates. During the 1980s, it increased in France and the US following the surge in real interest rates and growing indebtedness. In the 1990s, lowered interest rates along with a revival of economic growth allowed a decrease of this ratio despite rising debt (Figure 20, left). Since the late 1990s, interest rates have remained low, with two phases of marked decreases following the financial crises of 2001 and 2008. Figure 20 (right) shows us that in the early 2000s, the first decrease in interest rates allowed the weight of interest payments in the US and the UK to stabilise, despite rapidly rising indebtedness, and a continuous reduction where debt stabilised in Japan and Germany. Conversely, in the Anglo-Saxon countries, the accelerating indebtedness and climbing interest rates following 2006 translated into a rise in finance's drain on incomes – well above 10 per cent at its peak, which triggered the financial crash when subprime borrowers appeared unable to stomach this growing burden. However, the main lesson of this graph is that households pay a very significant amount of their income to financial institutions because they are in debt: 5 to 8 per cent of their disposable income, depending on the country concerned. Profits upon alienation are thus a category whose importance to the overall dynamic of capitalism cannot be neglected.

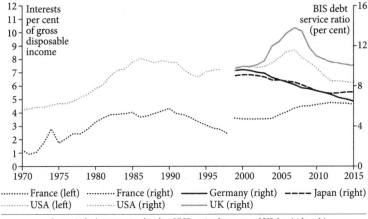

Figure 20: Debt service by households and NPIHS

At the socio-political level, household indebtedness feeds an immediately antagonistic relation between creditors and wage-earners/borrowers. However, this relation struggles to express itself, since unlike the wage relation it *a priori* sets each individual household against its creditors in an isolated and not collective manner. Nonetheless, in the countries most affected by the bursting of the real-estate bubble, the spike in evictions did make a common experience partly visible: the Spanish *Plataforma de Afectados por la Hipoteca* and the 'Strike Debt' movement in the United States thus managed to build the beginnings of a social mobilisation around this theme.

Profiting politically from public debt

The crisis has also spread to debt and the legitimacy of debt. In a work that has made a considerable impact, the anarchist anthropologist David Graeber tries to challenge the association between debt and blame and puts forward a proposal for a 'jubilee' for both international and consumer debt.[5] Since the 1980s, NGOs and social movements – for instance, the Committee for the Abolition of the Third World

---

5   David Graeber, *Debt: The First 5,000 Years*, New York: Melville House, 2011.

Debt – have mainly posed the problem of public debt in terms of the relations between global North and global South. However, as we showed in Chapter 3, over the last four decades the weight of public debt has also considerably increased in the countries of the North. With the Eurozone crisis and the austerity policies implemented in the name of debt reduction, debt has also become an important political question in Europe.[6] An in-depth debt-audit study undertaken in France has elaborated arguments challenging the legitimacy of debt.[7] But what is this all about?

> The public debt becomes one of the most powerful levers of primitive accumulation. As with the stroke of an enchanter's wand, it endows barren money with the power of breeding and thus turns it into capital, without the necessity of its exposing itself to the troubles and risks inseparable from its employment in industry or even in usury. The state creditors actually give nothing away, for the sum lent is transformed into public bonds, easily negotiable, which go on functioning in their hands just as so much hard cash would.[8]

In a few words, Marx captured the essence of public debt. It is an extremely liquid and almost risk-free asset. Historically, it has served as the raw material for the accumulation of great masses of financial and industrial private capital, and it remains the platform on which the scaffolding of the most complex financial packages is built. Marx's reference to the role of public debt in the primitive accumulation of capital points to an important course of reflection. It counts this mechanism among the extra-economic means presiding over the beginnings of accumulation, which have persisted throughout the course of capitalist development – what David Harvey calls accumulation by dispossession.[9]

The interest on public debt is not part of the surplus-value

---

6   François Chesnais, *Les dettes illégitimes: quand les banques font main basse sur les politiques publiques*, Paris: Raisons d'agir, 2011.

7   Michel Husson et al., 'Que faire de la dette? Un audit de la dette publique de la France', france.attac.org, 2014.

8   Karl Marx, *Capital*, Vol. I, Mineola, NY: Dover, 2011, p. 827.

9   David Harvey, *The New Imperialism*, Oxford: Oxford University Press, 2005.

extracted from the production process, nor is it directly drawn from household income; rather, it comes from political operations feeding revenue flow. These operations include capturing fiscal receipts by raising taxes, lowering public spending, privatisations and issuing new bonds. In the United States, the share of government bonds held by the richest 1 per cent rose from 16 per cent to more than 40 per cent between 1970 and 2010. Their share of federal interest payments has followed a similar pattern. As Sandy Hager shows, since tax deductions are insufficiently redistributive, the interest on public debt has contributed to concentrating income among the richest 1 per cent.[10] This empirical study is an important focus of contemporary debates, including in so far as it relates to Keynesian authors' propensity to favour public indebtedness. As far as I know, there is no equivalent work regarding European countries. The study underlines that without the introduction of increasingly progressive taxation and/or expenditure, growing debt will contribute to aggravating socio-economic inequalities. The sums at stake are considerable: in France during the 2000s, interest represented a 10 to 12 per cent share of all state spending.[11]

The conflictual social relation associated with public indebtedness sets the political community – as represented by governments – directly in confrontation with its creditors. Of course, when the growth rate is higher than the interest rate, public deficits do not aggravate indebtedness. But the liberalisation and internationalisation of the public debt offers markets the possibility of strangling public finances by increasing interest rates whenever they doubt a state's capacity to implement policies that will guarantee them the expected repayments and returns. Having already recurred throughout the financial crises in peripheral countries, this same dynamic also led to the European crisis of 2010–12. Thus, the sovereignty of markets steals a march on the sovereignty of peoples.[12] However, history is pockmarked with unilateral

---

10   Sandy Hager, 'America's real debt dilemma', *Review of Capital as Power*, 1:1 (2013), 41–62.

11   Muriel Pucci and Bruno Tinel, 'Réductions d'impôts et dette publique en France', *Revue de l'OFCE*, 116:1 (2011), 116–48.

12   Wolfgang Streeck, 'Les marchés et les peuples: capitalisme démocratique et intégration européenne', *New Left Review*, 73, January–February 2012.

debt cancellations, for example those made by absolutist monarchs, the Bolshevik revolutionaries or, to a lesser extent, the Ecuadorian and Argentinian governments of the 2000s. In their different ways, each of these cases reminds us that, in the last instance, the public debt relation is politically determined, and governments can put an end to it by simple decree.

The interest drawn from surplus-value in productive sectors

The third type of interest represents a part of the surplus-value generated by productive activities. The active fraction of capital which operates the productive and commercial valorisation process thus tends to enter into opposition with its creditors, as the interest it pays is subtracted from the profits it generates. However, we should not exaggerate this tension. The relation between loan capital and industrial and commercial capital is not just a zero-sum game. Outside of periods of crisis, the profit rate tends to be higher than the interest rate, and this implies that capitalists engaged in the real economy can improve the profitability of their own funds through a leverage effect. Indebtedness thus serves commercial and productive capital as a means of increasing its profitability.

A firm's indebtedness level is determined both by the growth of its expected profitability and by the evaluation of its risks. Indeed, taking on debts not only *increases* profitability, it also increases its *variability*. The expected advantages of the leverage effect are inverted when the firm's performance deteriorates or when interest rates increase. Indebtedness becomes a critical variable when profits collapse or interest rates rise, because it increases the risk of bankruptcy. One example that illustrates this relation is the FED's 1979 decision to abruptly increase its rates, which very rapidly affected worldwide borrowing conditions. In the countries of the global South, this resulted in a debt crisis, with Mexico's suspension of payments in 1982 firing the starting pistol. In the countries of the global North, this same rate increase had the effect of precipitating a fall in profits and a proliferation of bankruptcies. This shock also had repercussions for workers, by way of the wage restraints and waves of lay-offs that ultimately allowed the restoration of profitability. In sum, capital invested in the production process stands in oppositional relation to loan capital. Yet this opposition does not have a straightforwardly antagonistic character, since indebtedness can also sustain company owners' own remuneration. Loan capital also indirectly affects workers. After all, when financing conditions deteriorate, workers are the first to be exposed to the firm's increased vulnerability.

DIVIDENDS *QUA* DEDUCTION FROM CAPITALIST SURPLUS-VALUE

The profit that remains after interest is paid assumes an additional financial form on account of the dividends paid to shareholders. As early as the nineteenth century, the creation of joint-stock companies led to a pooling of capitals, which allowed the financing of large enterprises – notably the railways – to surpass the limitations of individually accumulated capitals. What was then a new form of organisation has now become the dominant one. It implies a separation between ownership and control,[13] and foregrounds the impersonal and autonomous character of capital's drive to accumulate. However, it does not take away the social embodiment of capital in relatively circumscribed groups of individuals, because the class borders between those who own capital and those who do not remain very much in place, even if the development of employee share-ownership, pension funds and even mutual investment funds does tend to blur the lines. We should also note that this new form of organisation helps accentuate the hierarchy among capital owners, because the big shareholders monopolise the capacity to influence company management, to the detriment of the minority shareholders. As Hilferding emphasises, 'The capitalists form an association in the direction of which most of them have no say.'[14] This phenomenon is aggravated yet further by the networks of cross-share ownership and holdings, today driving an extreme centralisation of capitalist power. We can observe that, on the eve of the current crisis, just 147 companies concentrated some 40 per cent of the

<hr />

13   Adolf Augustus Berle and Gardiner Coit Means, *The Modern Corporation and Private Property*, New York: Macmillan, 1932.

14   Rudolf Hilferding, *Finance Capital*, London: Taylor and Francis, 1990, p. 127.

value of all multinationals, and even these were themselves dominated by a core of eighteen financial entities.[15]

Ultimately, the opposition between owners and managers – the focus of the literature devoted to corporate governance – ought not to be exaggerated. Senior executives are most often also shareholders and partly remunerated in the form of shares and stock-options, not to mention the shareholder role they take on in the name of the companies they manage. Moreover, much as in the case of creditors, what is at stake here is the overall level of exploitation – that is, the division between wages and profits. The effect is that the power relations between owners and managers also tend to have repercussions on employees.

Shareholders and creditors contribute to financing capitalist activity by making their idle funds available in exchange for remuneration. On the one hand, the difference between the two owes to the fact that shareholders have engaged their capital over what is, formally speaking, an indefinite period. On the other hand, it owes to the fact that their remuneration in the form of dividends involves an element of discretion, which is not the case with interest payments. Interest and dividends take up part of a company's profits. Moreover, financial markets make shareholders' positions liquid. This allows them easily to withdraw the financial capital they have invested, just as the lender gets back his principal upon its due date. In parallel to this, debt securities themselves largely become liquid. Thus, ultimately, we can consider the interest on company bonds as well as dividends as a kind of rentier income, if by that we mean the financial revenues that result from the simple making available of money-capital. They capture part of the surplus-value realised in the productive sphere, but without the counterpart of having any major implication in the company's risks.

---

15   Stefania Vitali, James B. Glattfelder and Stefano Battiston, 'The network of global corporate control', *PloS one*, 6:10 (2011); Gérard Duménil and Dominique Lévy, *La grande bifurcation: en finir avec le néolibéralisme*, Paris: La Découverte, 2014.

CAPITAL GAINS

The prices of shares and tradable debts fluctuate just like the prices of other types of real assets like real estate or raw materials. This variability opens the way to another type of financial profit that at first sight seems more difficult to grasp: capital gains. These are the profits that result from the difference between an equity's purchase price and its sale price. Speculators are exclusively oriented toward this type of profit.

Unlike the interest and dividends that firms pay, this type of profit does not draw at all on company profits. It is realised on the financial markets alone, when whoever holds a security manages to sell it on for a higher price than they bought it for. Formally speaking, the profit thus derives from the idle money that the buyer wishes to invest in this equity. It results from a change in market agents' evaluation of future returns and the risks associated with the asset concerned. As we have seen, this is a self-referential evaluation. However, it is defined – within the limits of plausibility – relatively autonomously of the fundamental value that results from the anticipated income associated with the risk/returns pairing. In short, even though capital gains are real, they result from variations in the value of fictitious capital. Whatever the type of assets under consideration, capital gains result from a zero-sum game among the various participants on the market: the fictitious capital accumulated through price rises becomes a reality for a given vendor when a buyer on the market himself takes over this fiction. These capital gains are nil, overall, if the surplus-value realised by some actors is matched by lossmaking sales by others. If they are positive, overall, in a given period, this is because the relevant asset market has attracted more available money-capital. This additional capital flow can come either from other less favoured asset markets, from a decline in bank savings, from an increase in overall savings, from the import of capitals or, finally, from an increase in the banking credit devoted to financial operations.

We need to introduce two more specific considerations here, bringing greater nuance to this general picture. The first concerns the profits realised when an asset is first offered on the market. Hilferding provided an in-depth demonstration of this one-time profit, which he called 'founder's profit'. This comes from the operation transforming the initially invested capital, financed by loans remunerated at the interest rate or by fresh cash or asset inflows, into productive capital remunerated at the rate of profit. Indeed, when a company is founded its initial assets and activities are financed by what its founders contribute but also by debts. Its share price when it arrives on the stock market results from a completely different calculation: the capitalisation of anticipated profits. The sum thus levied is dependent on the expected profit rate. Since, in normal periods, this rate will be higher than the interest rate, the amount thus obtained exceeds the debts taken on by its founders. This offers them an exceptional profit.

To explain how this mechanism works, we can take the example of Facebook's initial public offering (IPO) on the stock market on 18 May 2012.[16] The firm decided to put 421 million shares on sale that day, at the price of $38 each. This represented 15 per cent of the company's capital, or a sum of $16bn, with the company's total capitalisation amounting to 2.8 billion shares, or $106bn. These shares had previously been held by its founders, company executives and a few investors. Mark Zuckerberg himself sold 30 million shares for a capital gain of $1.15bn. He held on to around 509 million shares, around 20 per cent of the total. The moment Facebook was listed, this represented a sum of $19bn. We need to look further back in time to get an idea of the founder's profit realised in this operation. In 2006, *Businessweek* estimated the company's value at $2bn. We can take this figure as an approximation – an exaggerated one – of the capital engaged in the firm. If the 15 per cent sold during its IPO represented an invested capital of $300m, the founder's profit realised in the IPO amounts to $15.7bn. But since the shares are listed on the stock exchange, even those parts not put on sale during the IPO can now also be circulated. Thus the total amount of founder's profit corresponding to this new valuation is some $104.6bn! As for Zuckerberg himself, he collected an effective profit of $995m through the IPO and a potential profit – considering the shares he did keep – of some $18.7bn. The thirty-three investment banks that

16   Bernard Condon, 'Questions and answers on blockbuster Facebook IPO', bigstory. ap.org, 17 May 2012.

organised its listing also collected a substantial profit in the form of a commission of around 3 per cent, or $480m.

The other element that needs considering is the role of the public authorities, as Minsky indicates. In so far as central banks do not intervene, capital gains result from a zero-sum game within the financial community. Yet monetary policy plays a central role in determining assets' prices: if interest rates rise, prices fall; conversely, a policy of low interest rates helps keep prices high. At an even more immediate level, quantitative easing by central banks serves to push up prices – both directly through asset purchases and indirectly by prompting investors to move to riskier and more remunerative asset classes. This allows the realisation of fictitious-capital gains that would not otherwise have existed. Of course, central bank interventions are but one of the factors determining the level of market capitalisation. Yet, in the post-crisis context, they are an element of crucial importance.

Figure 21 illustrates this phenomenon. It sets in parallel the evolution of the main central banks' assets and market capitalisation. In this regard, there is a sharp divide between the US and Japan, on the one hand, and the Eurozone on the other. While, in the former cases, central bank actions favoured an extremely strong rebound on the stock markets, the ECB's more timorous intervention – especially

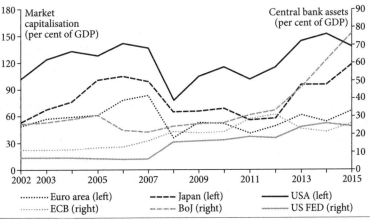

Source: Author's computations based on World Bank (WDI), OECD and national central banks

Figure 21: Market capitalisation and central bank assets

when it contracted its balance sheet in 2013 and 2014 – led to a much weaker recovery, and its more recent asset-buying programme seems to have had weaker effects. However, what Figure 21 mostly emphasises is the fact that central bank balance sheets play a decisive role in sustaining market capitalisation in the post-Lehman world. These balance sheets are committed at levels well above the pre-crisis norm.

FINANCIAL INSTITUTIONS' PROFITS

Let us now examine one last type of financial profit, namely the profits of the companies fulfilling the role of financial intermediaries. This includes the income stemming from the operations they conduct on their own account (dividends, interests and capital gains) but also the profits generated by the activities they realise for their clients.

These institutions' most immediately tangible source of revenue comes from the fees and commissions they charge. The operations concerned are extremely diverse. To take just a few examples, they range from the commissions the big investment banks award themselves when they are conducting mergers and acquisitions to account management fees and the commissions commercial banks take on cash machine withdrawals or currency exchange operations.

This second type of revenue is at the heart of financial intermediaries' activity. From banks to mortgage loan insurance, from exchange operations to export credit, and from consumer credit companies to pension savings, in financial institutions the same principle is always at work: transforming debts' qualities and maturities such that the available money-capital can meet the demand for finance. For example, taking premiums from their clients, insurers build up a portfolio of assets. They invest this while deducting the pay outs they have to make. For insurance activity to remain stable and reliable, these assets must exceed the present value of the estimated cost of the pay outs. The same general principle also applies in pension funds and banking activities. The profits these financial institutions generate thus result from their capacity to achieve valorisation rates for their assets superior to the dynamic evolution of their liabilities.

The present-day measurement of future liabilities is fundamental in this regard. It is uncertain in two senses. The first uncertainty corresponds to the evaluation of future liabilities (for insurers, the risk of accidents; for pension funds, the payment of pensions, etc.). Without doubt, it is very difficult to evaluate this uncertainty, though these actors can mark it out in broad terms on the basis of past experience. Conversely, the second uncertainty is a systemic one: it is situated precisely in the discount rates used to evaluate these future liabilities' present value. The higher these rates, the lower the present value of present liabilities, and vice versa.

As a general rule, under the new financial accounting norms the discount rates given for the long-term liabilities of actors like insurers and pension funds are equivalent to the return on AA-rated bonds (typical of long-term government bonds). The problem is that when interest rates fall – as in recent years with negative official deposit facility rates in Japan and the Eurozone, among others – returns on safe assets plunge, leaving these actors with rising liabilities and no corresponding upswing in their receipts. This difficulty in managing risks is a real conundrum.[17] With more than $13bn of assets traded at negative rates, including 55 per cent of public debt securities in the Eurozone, for many institutions the situation is becoming critical. Banks and insurance companies are being hard hit, but the weakest link is pension funds. Several are considering downward readjustments of previously defined payments as the industry faces a perilous financial situation across the Western world.[18] Moreover, the constant re-evaluation of liabilities and resources drives these financial actors toward pro-cyclical behaviours that contribute to destabilising financial dynamics.

Banking and insurance are tightly regulated fields. This owes firstly to the fact that the search for profit through financial intermediation

---

17 Iain Clacher and Peter Moizer, 'Accounting for Pensions', Leeds University Business School, plsa.co.uk, 2011; Clara Severinson and Juan Yermo, *The Effect of Solvency Regulations and Accounting Standards on Long-term Investing: Implications for Insurers and Pension Funds*, OECD Publishing, 2012.

18 'Negative interest rates "poison" German pension funds', FT.com, 15 May 2016; 'UK ministers urged to delay further rises in pension contributions', FT.com, 22 September 2016; 'The US public pensions crisis "is really hard to fix"', FT.com, 1 May 2016.

spontaneously leads to the emergence of Ponzi pyramid schemes, and secondly to the fact that these intermediation activities fulfil indispensable societal functions. The proper functioning of the payments system, of pensions systems and of insurance – and indeed, bank deposit integrity – are imperative to contemporary capitalism's reproduction. Regulation's capacity to head off risks has been greatly weakened by the liberalisation of finance and the development of shadow banking, described above. However, as the public authorities' energetic action to save the financial system in 2007–8 demonstrated, the need to guarantee continuity in its functions is still just as pressing. These explicit or implicit public guarantees very much work to the financial institutions' benefit, allowing them to finance themselves at a lower cost. They thus constitute a sort of subsidy.

Such public subsidies have a far from negligible impact on financial institutions' profits. A study commissioned by the Green group in the European Parliament offered a synthesis of academic works on this subject, focusing on the continent's big banks.[19] It concluded that in 2012 there was an implicit subsidy of some €233bn – 1.8 per cent of European GDP – and similar amounts for each year from 2007 onward. The IMF provides further proof that the implicit subsidy to the big banks is of this order, evaluating it at $300bn in Europe in 2012 and $70bn in the US.[20] The first lesson we can take from this is that big banks would record considerable losses if it were not for such underlying state support. It subsidises their profits. The second lesson is that this also has a cost for the public authorities. In moments of crisis, there is a direct drain on state budgets as public guarantees are activated and state money flows into bank coffers. But this is also true in normal periods, since the finance markets factor these liabilities into the interest rates they apply to the public debt. These government guarantees thus benefit finance in two distinct ways: they allow finance not only to enjoy lower interest rates, but also to inflict higher rates on states themselves.

19   Alexander Kloeck, 'Implicit subsidies in the EU banking sector', study commissioned by the Green/EFA group in the European Parliament, greens-efa.eu, January 2014.

20   IMF, 'How big is the implicit subsidy for banks considered too important to fail?', *Global Financial Stability Report 2014*, Washington DC: IMF.

Calculating these implicit subsidies is hardly unproblematic, since it relies on what are rather precarious present-value calculations. But it certainly does underline one thing: given that public guarantees are indispensable to a large part of financial institutions' activities, it is wholly illegitimate that the profits resulting from these activities are privatised.

FINANCIAL PROFITS' SOCIO-POLITICAL CONTENT

An examination of financial revenues allows us to provide a summary representation (Table 2) which shows that there is no coincidence between the forms of these revenues and their sources. The different types of financial profit have five distinct origins, which in turn each correspond to different socio-political contradictions.

Deductions from company profits are based on the repartition of the surplus-value extracted from production activities, which is divided between productive capital and financial capital. Capital gains are partly based on a *zero-sum game* between participants on the financial markets and the providers of disposable money-capital. *Founder's profit* also corresponds to a game that plays out internally to capital. The offering of a company on the stock market allows its creators – as well as the banks organising this operation – to pocket profits corresponding to the gap between the price of the firm's assets and its market valorisation based on the capitalisation of its future profits.

Profits upon alienation result from a radically different logic, indeed one that recalls pre-capitalist forms of revenue associated with debt. They represent a direct drain on individuals' incomes, regardless of any kind of control over the production process itself.

The final category corresponds to what I would propose we call *political profits*. These profits result from a flow of revenue toward finance, mediated by public institutions. These political profits themselves break down into two sub-categories. They result from both the interest on government bonds and the flows of interest payments stemming from financial stability policies. These latter are the policies of the lender of last resort: that is to say, the whole set of guarantees and aid measures from which the financial sector profits so greatly. These include direct forms of socialising losses (we need only think of the recapitalisation of the US insurer AIG, the DEXIA bank in France and Benelux, or the nationalisation of the Northern Rock bank in the UK). Contrary to the general view, I do not see financial stability as a public good from which everyone benefits. That is not to deny the negative externalities associated with financial instability that do affect all actors. Yet it is worth emphasising that state action in favour of financial stability above all benefits financial intermediaries and actors seeking to realise capital gains. Financial stability policies validate fictitious capital's mounting valorisation on the finance markets, even when the autonomous interplay of market actors would have led to its abrupt devalorisation. These policies also have a social cost, since they translate into either an increase in public debt (or of its cost, by way of increased interest rates) or the issuing of an excess amount of currency.

These different sources of financial revenue correspond to different socio-political contradictions. We will emphasise just two of them. The particular logic of *profits upon alienation* mainly stems from waged households' debt relation. Indebtedness sets them in opposition to financial institutions, indeed in a strictly antagonistic relationship, in so far as they are subject to a straightforward deduction from their income without any possibility of exercising a leverage effect to increase their income. The relation that results from *political profits* is less immediate but equally conflictual. Through this relationship, the financial community as a whole comes to form a homogeneous body confronting the rest of society on such burning questions as the public debt and financial stability.

This description of financial profits, their origins and the contradictions associated with them provides us with a basis for thinking through financialisation's economic and socio-political effects. We should begin by casting aside the idea that financial activities are purely 'predatory'. It is true that their remuneration exclusively results from deductions from the revenues of production activities, households or public institutions. Nonetheless, financial activities do also contribute to capital circulation, for they prevent disposable funds from laying idle; allow the creation of credit money; and encourage

Table 2: The forms and socio-political content of financial profits

	Social relation	Recipient	Origin	Socio-political contradiction
Interest	Debt	Creditors	Deduction from company profit	Creditors / capital engaged in production / employees
			Profits upon alienation	Creditor / individual debtor
			Political profit	Creditor / political community
Dividends	Property	Shareholders	Deduction from company profits	Shareholders / managers / employees
Capital gains			Zero-sum game among market participants with disposable money-capital	None
	Speculation	Asset sellers	Founder's profit	Entrepreneurs / shareholders
			Political profits	Financial system / political community (financial stability)
Fees for managing financial flows			Deduction from company profits	Financial institutions / capital invested in production and trade
	Trading money	Financial institutions	Profits upon alienation	Financial institutions / depositors, the insured, borrowers
			Political profits	Financial system / political community (financial stability)

capital's expansion through the advance financing of new productive activities. Financial institutions and asset markets also play an essential cognitive role: they guide capital flows by selecting the sectors with the most promising profitability and identifying others where profitability is declining. They thus constitute the real 'control room' of economic development. As Lapavitsas emphasises, finance 'acts as the nerves and brains of the capitalist economy; it is the social entity that turns the marshalling of spare resources by society into an integral whole'.[21] Finance is thus fundamentally ambivalent. This is what Figure 22 demonstrates. It is split between the predatory logic inherent in its incapacity to generate value by itself and, on the other hand, its role in organising capital accumulation, which favours innovation. It stands at a more abstract level than the developments that preceded it, for it is no longer based on particular incarnations of the different types of financial income flows, but aims directly to model the socio-economic dynamics which are at their origin.

Its *innovating* element poses no particular difficulties: in allowing good capital allocation, finance drains available resources toward those

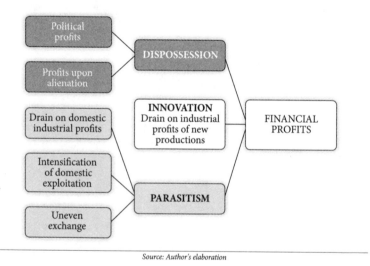

Source: Author's elaboration

Figure 22: Socio-economic processes at the roots of financial profits

---

21   Lapavitsas, *Profiting Without Producing*, p. 201.

areas where they can most profitably be put to use. It draws its remuneration from the increased profits associated with the emergence of new production activities. Finance's *dispossessing* aspect echoes the concept David Harvey mobilises in his characterisation of the forms of profit that do not result from exploiting labour.[22] This aspect of finance involves the various different modalities by which it extracts income from populations, either indirectly – through *political profits* – or directly – through *profits upon alienation*. In this context, the concept of *parasitism* refers to the revenues deducted from company profits by entities which themselves stand entirely outside of the production process. These deductions from company profits correspond to two different configurations. The first kind are a simple deduction from company profits, coming at the cost of the company's capacity to finance investment. In the second case, finance can draw profits from an increase in the company's own profits. This can result from either a rise in the rate of exploitation of its employees or a relation of unequal exchange between the companies strongly connected to finance and those that are not. Of course, this latter question also has an international dimension. The question of *unequal exchange* corresponds to the capacity of firms in the global North to remunerate financial actors thanks to gains from asymmetrical market relations with their suppliers, in particular those in the countries of the global South.

Innovation, dispossession and parasitism: such are the social logics that underpin financial profits.

---

22   Harvey, *The New Imperialism*.

CHAPTER SEVEN

Finance in Service of the Metamorphoses of Capital

Our description of the rise of fictitious capital and the different forms of financial profits has allowed us to define the contours of financialisation. Now we must try to interpret it. With that purpose in mind, we will look at authors who have contextualised financialisation amid the general dynamic of capitalism and who see today's convulsions in a rather optimistic light. Unlike neoclassical economists, they do not think that the markets allocate capital efficiently. However, they treat financialisation as an institutional arrangement that ultimately does assure the transition from one phase of capitalist development to another, notwithstanding its own instability. This argument also has two variants. One version emphasises that knowledge and the immaterial have assumed unprecedented importance in the contemporary economy and that this implies new modalities of evaluation and valorisation. Meanwhile, the second maintains that the phases of financial hegemony always accompany the emergence of new technical-economic paradigms.

Toward Cognitive Capitalism?

> Not to withdraw from the process, but to go further,
> to 'accelerate the process', as Nietzsche put it.
>
> Deleuze and Guattari[1]

Information technologies clearly mark an epochal change. Personal computers and their networking have penetrated all social spheres, transforming both the organisational forms of trade and production and ways of life in the wider sense. Does this mutation coincide with the advent of a new capitalism? This, in any case, is the position of those

---

1 Gilles Deleuze and Félix Guattari, *Anti-Oedipus*, London: Athlone, 1984.

who maintain that the increased power of knowledge and the imma-terial has shaken up the very principles of the economy's functioning.

We find the boldest version of this argument among the defend-ers of the 'cognitive capitalism' thesis. This theoretical proposition is linked to Italian *operaismo*, a current that sees proletarian struggles as the motor of capitalist development.[2] The Fordist-era mass-work-er's resistance against the alienation of assembly-line labour and the great international wave of mobilisations in 1968 were the origin of a systemic transformation. This transformation manifested itself in expanded access to secondary and higher education, new forms of labour that increasingly valorised autonomy, and finally the rise of digital technologies. These struggles were partly victorious. The aspi-ration for the liberation of each person's creative forces combined with technological developments and resulted in a new capitalism centred on immaterial labour and principally oriented toward the accumula-tion and valorisation of knowledges.[3]

This would mean an unprecedented transformation – a complete paradigm shift. According to this narrative, knowledge is becoming the principal source of value creation as the immaterial substitutes for the material as the central object of economic activity. This would mean the old questions of scarcity and diminishing returns being reduced to a secondary level of importance, with a logic of increasing returns now instead predominating.

This logic is well known in the context of cultural goods. Let us take the example of *Grand Theft Auto V*, a video game that came out in autumn 2013. Its development and marketing costs amounted to a record $267m, and these were fixed costs. Once the game itself had been produced, making an extra unit (a disc and its box, or a down-load) brought almost no extra expense. In other words, the greater the number of units sold – as it happens, the game shifted 16 million copies on the day it was released, for a sum of $800m! – the lower the average cost per unit. The same is true of books and films but also, at

---

2   Michael Hardt and Antonio Negri, *Empire*, Cambridge, MA: Harvard University Press, 2000, p. 261.

3   Yann Moulier Boutang, *Le capitalisme cognitif: la nouvelle grande transformation*, Paris: Éditions Amsterdam, 2007, pp. 94–5.

least partly, of industrial products with major R&D costs or for which brand reputation is of decisive importance. In sum, we are seeing the immaterial becoming increasingly important to production. Producing the first unit of a commodity incorporating new knowledges is very expensive, but the cost of the additional units is almost nil.

This turn toward the immaterial has profound consequences. Firstly, it is difficult to ensure the market valorisation of immaterial products by preventing them being used for free. Yet the immaterial use-value that has been produced has to be kept within its commodity 'container'. Hence the development of a juridical arsenal for the protection of intellectual property, DRM (digital rights management) measures seeking to prevent the copying of digital works, and Terminator technologies that make GM plants sterile in order to prevent the reuse of their second generation. The pre-emptive destruction of use-value (forbidding or restricting the use of goods whose consumption by one agent does not prevent it also being consumed by other agents) with the objective of preserving a product's market value also poses the question of the obsolescence of the commodity form.[4] This tension gives fresh present-day relevance to Marx's famous statement that

> At a certain stage of development, the material productive forces of society come into conflict with the existing relations of production or – this merely expresses the same thing in legal terms – with the property relations within the framework of which they have operated hitherto. From forms of development of the productive forces these relations turn into their fetters. Then begins an era of social revolution. The changes in the economic foundation lead sooner or later to the transformation of the whole immense superstructure.[5]

The commodification of knowledges by means of patents today serves to limit investment and hobble innovation.[6] This is true of the coun-

---

4 Sébastien Chauvin and Olga Sezneva, 'Has capitalism gone virtual? Content containment and the obsolescence of the commodity', *Critical Historical Studies*, 1:1 (2014), 125–50.

5 Karl Marx, 'Preface to A Contribution to the Critique of Political Economy', in *Selected Writings*, Indianapolis: Hackett, 1994, p. 211.

6 Benjamin Coriat and Olivier Weinstein, 'Patent regimes, firms and the

tries of the South, which have found themselves forbidden access to technologies protected by property rights, or else allowed such access only at prohibitive costs. But it is also the case in rich countries, where firms are generalising the use of defensive patenting strategies to stop competition developing. Take the example of the war between Apple and Samsung – during which the former tried to enforce a patent on the rounded corners of its tablets – or even the battle that Myriad Genetics waged over more than a decade to defend its rights over the genetic codes used in breast cancer prevention tests. The lawsuits it brought shackled the work of research bodies like the Curie Institute and imposed prohibitive test costs on patients. The US Supreme Court ultimately ruled against Myriad in June 2013, judging that a DNA strand present in its natural state could not be patented.

The contradiction between property and use is just one of the numerous problems posed by the increased importance of the immaterial in the knowledge economy. According to those who argue that there is a new 'cognitive capitalism', the immaterial is shaking up the division of labour, the modalities of labour exploitation, and the perspectives for emancipation. Logically enough, this has given rise to major controversies over the empirical and political relevance of this thesis.[7] This is not the place to go back over these debates. What interests us here are the close links that this approach claims to have identified between the immaterial economy and finance. This is why Yann Moulier Boutang argues:

> In the global functioning of a profoundly reworked capitalism the rise of the immaterial (intangible accounting items) and the growing importance of externalities make the conventions and institutional

---

commodification of knowledge', *Socio-Economic Review*, 10:2 (2012), 267–92; Ugo Pagano and Maria Alessandra Rossi, 'The crash of the knowledge economy', *Cambridge Journal of Economics*, 33:4 (2009), 665–83; Ugo Pagano, 'The crisis of intellectual monopoly capitalism', *Cambridge Journal of Economics*, 38:6 (2014), 1409–29.

7   See in particular Michel Husson, 'Sommes-nous entrés dans le "capitalisme cognitif"?', *Critique Communiste*, Nos. 169–70 (2003); E.M. Mouhoud, 'Marchandisation de la connaissance ou main invisible du communisme?', in Pierre Dardot, Christian Laval and E.M. Mouhoud (eds), *Sauver Marx?: empire, multitude, travail immatériel*, Paris: La Découverte, 2007.

arrangements of Fordist capitalism redundant. Finance thus proves to be the only appropriate means of 'governing' cognitive capitalism's intrinsic instability.[8]

In this argument, the gap between firms' accounting value and their stock-market capitalisation is a manifestation of finance markets' capacity to valorise intangible assets like R&D potential, portfolios of patents, organisation, lists of suppliers and clients, and brand image – all of which contribute to future profit flows. Dominique Plihon and El Mouhoub Mouhoud identify this same idea in less grandiloquent terms: 'the institutions of a capitalism dominated by finance largely seek to regulate the triple problem of valorising, appropriating and managing the risks posed by the knowledge economy, in the interests of the owners of finance capital'.[9] According to this analysis, market finance is better able than banks to assure companies' financing. This owes to its greater capacity to get to grips with uncertainties in the returns on intangible assets and, in consequence, to evaluate the value of firms.

Without doubt, the returns associated with intangible assets are particularly uncertain. Profits become very volatile when fixed costs are high, for if the costs of production are essentially incurred before the product goes to market no *ex post* adjustment is possible. Again taking the example of a video game (or a big Hollywood production, or a piece of software), there will be considerable profits if the product gets an audience; conversely, it is impossible to limit losses by reducing production levels if the public turns its nose up at it. This problem of irrecoverable costs is similarly posed for industrial products requiring major R&D expenditure.

A look at start-ups helps us to understand the radical uncertainty associated with innovation. Financing a new firm engaged in the exclusive development of a new technology poses particular problems, in so far as while there may be huge potential profits, the probability of failure is also very high. Indeed, this is the reason why some investors – venture capitalists – have specialised in financing this type of

---

8   Moulier Boutang, *Le capitalisme cognitif*, p. 201.

9   E.M. Mouhoud and Dominique Plihon, *Le savoir et la finance liaisons dangereuses au cœur du capitalisme contemporain*, Paris: La Découverte, 2009, p. 117.

operation. This also allows finance to appear in a more intrepid guise. Yet despite its striking appearance, venture capital remains of very minor importance relative to all financing activities. Investments in innovative start-ups certainly have played a decisive role in the IT and biotechnologies booms. But they represent only a rather limited phenomenon, and cannot explain the masses of finance that financialisation has mobilised.

If we look at Mouhoud and Plihon's argument more closely, they do not limit themselves to questions regarding finance's relations with immaterial labour and innovation. They argue that 'the stock market makes it possible to resolve the problem of the so-called "irreversibility" of investments in productive capital, making the equities whose exchange it organises available at each moment, and thus liquid'.[10] Since stock-market liquidity makes financial investments reversible – at least outside of periods of crisis – it plays a role in reducing uncertainty. This allows entrepreneurs to find capital holders who accept the risk of financing what are very much irreversible investments. While this argument is not wrong on its own terms, its significance is considerably reduced by the fact – underlined by the authors – that over recent decades the markets have not played the role of financing the economy. Rather, net capital flows have passed from the non-financial sector to the finance markets, not the other way around. More fundamentally, the principle of uncertainty associated with irrecoverable costs is not particular to the knowledge economy. Rather, it is an old problem that just as much concerns the irreversibility effects associated with major investments in industry.[11] Already in their day, Hilferding and Minsky emphasised this same problem and its link with the financial system, even within a context radically different to that of market finance. Banks seek to prevent excessive competition devaluing investments, which could harm their clients' profitability and thus their capacity to reimburse the debt they owe them. Banks thus support the formation of cartels and privilege companies that enjoy greater market

---

10   Ibid., p. 124.

11   Bertrand Quelin and Laurent Benzoni, 'La concurrence oligopolistique: dynamique et instabilité', in Richard Arena et al. (eds), *Traité d'économie industrielle*, Paris: Economica, 1988, p. 485.

power.[12] In sum, the problem of financing specific investments is not particular to the knowledge economy, and nor does it necessarily have to be resolved by way of liberalised finance markets.

On the connected question of evaluating firms' value, Mouhoud and Plihon argue that bankers' accounting analysis tools are little able to account for firms' valorisation prospects and that this explains the growing recourse to financing via the finance markets. While they also criticise the deregulation of finance and the destabilising effects that follow from it, they nonetheless seem to accept the reforms to enterprises' accounting and financial norms (the IFRS norms). Yet these new norms base private accounting on the principle of *fair value* – an asset's market value at a given moment – as against the previous approach based on acquisition value (historical costs). After all, they explain, the market 'is able to take into account all the elements that accounting based on historical costs is not able to evaluate. It is on this basis that the stock market provides an answer to the problem of how to valorise a company's intangible assets'.[13]

Here Mouhoud and Plihon are doing nothing more than adopting Hayek's idea that the market is a process that reveals a dispersed knowledge – an idea that they apply to the particular case of financial markets and intangible assets. In this view, markets are best able to bring to light the information relevant to evaluating firms' profit prospects, given that they allow the encounter/comparison of a multitude of viewpoints. This information is by its very nature disseminated across social bodies. There are, however, two problems with this analysis. While the authors do refer to the mimetic polarisation that results from financial valorisation's self-referential character – as underlined by Keynes, Minsky and Orléan – they overlook the dynamic of the creation/preservation of fictitious capital, as well as the effect that speculative bubbles have in distorting information and driving bad capital allocation. Moreover, here too, they are clearly exaggerating the novelty of the difficulties of firm evaluation in the context of the knowledge

12   Piero Ferri and Hyman P. Minsky, 'Market processes and thwarting systems', Levi Economics Institute Working Paper No. 64, November 1991, pp. 16–17; Hilferding, *Finance Capital*.

13   Mouhoud and Plihon, *Le savoir et la finance liaisons dangereuses*, p. 40.

economy. If financing innovation does indeed pose a problem, there is no basis for considering this specific to our own time. On the contrary, it is a problematic that has periodically recurred throughout the history of capitalism.

THE ROLE OF FINANCE CAPITAL WHEN LONG WAVES CHANGE DIRECTION

Money was the dungheap in which grew the humanity of tomorrow ... Poisonous and destructive money became the ferment of all social vegetation, served as the necessary compost for the execution of the great works which would draw the nations nearer together and pacify the earth.

Zola, *Money*

Some might think that finance plays a role in regenerating capitalism. Yet the hypothesis that a phase of financial hegemony occurs in each period when a new technical-economic paradigm is established is doubtless on more solid ground than the hypothesis of the advent of a radically new type of capitalism. This is the position defended by the Venezuelan researcher Carlota Perez.[14] She has thus picked up the torch of a long tradition interested in the long-term movements of capitalism's dynamic – a tradition that itself dates back to the beginning of the last century.[15]

According to this type of approach, capitalist development does not obey any linear logic. Rather, it is punctuated by relatively regular cycles lasting several years, linked to the renewal of production facilities. But it also follows multi-decade shifts, during which a phase of expansion associated with the deployment of a new technological

---

14   Carlota Perez, 'The double bubble at the turn of the century: technological roots and structural implications', *Cambridge Journal of Economics*, 33:4 (2009), 779-805; 'Finance and technical change: a long-term view: research paper'.

15   The pioneering works in this domain – by Parvus, Van Gelderen and of course Nicolas Kondratieff – date back to the first third of the twentieth century. Joseph Schumpeter would discuss them at length. Major contributions in recent decades include works by Ernest Mandel, Éric Bosserelle and finally Chris Freeman and Francisco Louça. For a theoretical and historical perspective on this question, see Christopher Freeman and Francisco Louça, *As Time Goes By: From the Industrial Revolutions to the Information Revolution*, Oxford: Oxford University Press, 2001.

system is followed by a phase of decline when this system's propulsive force is exhausted, in turn allowing the seeds of a fresh wave of expansion to appear. Indeed, these shifts are long waves and not cycles, in the measure that the unleashing of a fresh wave of expansion is by no means inevitable. If the end of the expansive wave results from an exhaustion dynamic internal to this wave, there is nothing automatic about the way out of the depressive phase. According to Ernest Mandel, exogenous systemic shocks (wars, counter-revolutions, working-class defeats, the discovery of new resources) are necessary to alter conditions and fuel a rapid rise in profits, which will allow the system to take off again. But such events are contingent: their outcomes are decided outside of the strictly economic dynamic of the capital accumulation process itself.[16] Perez reformulates this idea of indeterminacy by arguing that the initiation of a new wave necessarily requires the institutional crystallisation of the social, political and cultural transformations allowing the economic potential of new technological developments to be concretised. She thus also borrows a concept of paradigms from the epistemology of Thomas Kuhn, emphasising the long gestation of system-level technical-economic transformations and the strong resistances they encounter.

But why is it that, in certain periods, technological innovations spread rapidly, indeed in bunches, whereas other eras are characterised by relative stagnation? After all, there is no *a priori* reason to expect that the manifestations of human ingenuity should be irregularly distributed across time. Perez proposes the following explanation: in a phase of expansion, innovations will struggle to find finance because the returns brought by the already established technologies are strong enough to absorb the available capitals. Conversely, when the deployment of these technologies reaches its limits – when a phase of expansion reaches its end – a significant mass of profits is available, yet the opportunities for profitable investments become rarer. The fall in profit rates then gives rise to an efficient reorganisation of the production system, during which the singularity of finance capital as distinct from industrial capital takes on its full importance.

---

16   Ernest Mandel, 'Explaining long waves of capitalist development', *Futures*, 13:4 (1981), 332–8.

Finance capital is not made up of material and immaterial assets directly engaged in production, but of idle money and securities. It is therefore less specialised and more flexible than industrial capital. It is far better able than the latter to set out in search of new types of investments as it turns away from activities whose yields are declining. Thus, projects that would have been ignored in the preceding period are now financed, whether they relate to new branches of activity or the modernisation of existing sectors. This is why innovations principally appear during phases of economic decline. Yet this is a profoundly unstable process.

First of all, the search for new profitable operations is not always crowned with success. Very many projects prove to be dead-ends, and only at the end of an economic selection process does a limited number of technologies emerge with the capacity to drive development. Subsequently, the success of a certain number of projects will itself initiate sharp financial shifts. The discovery of a new El Dorado excites passions and attracts ever more capitals, to the point that hopes for profits are disappointed. The decline phases of the cycle thus arrive at the turning point where bubbles turn into violent financial crises. These, in turn, depress production, as we can see in the cases of the canal mania in 1790s Great Britain, the bubble of speculation on railways at the end of the first half of the nineteenth century, and the scramble to invest in peripheral countries' infrastructure in the final quarter of that century. At that time, Paris's stock exchange – together with its London counterpart – was the epicentre of these international operations' financing. Such was the climate in which Aristide Saccard, the unscrupulous hero of Émile Zola's novel *Money*, launched a Universal Bank focused on investment in the Middle East. Through a public campaign, he manages to whip up a frenzy of speculation and attract small and middling savers' funds so that he can make his fortune again. In the twentieth century, the stock-market euphoria of the Roaring Twenties led to the Great Depression. Finally, in our own era, the dotcom bubble and the casino-finance bubble that immediately followed plunged us into the great recession.

The self-amplifying character of financial exuberance systematically leads to crashes and depressions. But these phases of major instability, most often associated with economic liberalisation taking place under the hegemony of finance capital, bequeath a dual inheritance – an inheritance for both production and politics. Firstly, the obsolete branches are eliminated or modernised, while the abundance of credit allows the infrastructure of a new technical-economic paradigm to establish itself. The economic and social violence associated with finance's hegemony then provokes a reaction in the social body itself, a Polanyian movement of resistance to commodification that opens the way to new socio-political compromises under the hegemony of productive capital. These compromises are characterised by the strengthening of state intervention and of the constraints imposed on markets, reflecting in a more or less deformed way the aspiration for greater social justice. Table 3 shows the place of these financial bubbles in the dynamic of the long waves that have taken place since the Industrial Revolution.

Of course, we could question this periodisation, for it does not do justice to the historical-geographic singularity of the moments it covers. There could be no consensus at this level of generalisation.[17] However, the schema that Carlota Perez proposes is of interest for our purposes because it shows that, even in its moments of excess, finance plays a cognitive role essential to economic reorganisation. In supporting attempts to unearth new opportunities for profit, it creates great instability, provokes depressions and increases socio-economic tensions. But, ultimately, it contributes to regenerating the system by abandoning declining sectors and encouraging the emergence of sectors bearing a fresh dynamism. In a context of decline, finance creates the conditions for the deployment of new productive forces. Nonetheless, the realisation of this potential requires institutional change of a socio-political character, whose outcome is contingent.

---

17 For example, Angus Maddison has proposed another temporal division of the successive phases of capitalist development, based on his analysis of long-term economic data. He places greater emphasis on institutional factors (the monetary regime, the fixing of wage-rates, the role of the state, the international system). See Angus Maddison, *Dynamic Forces in Capitalist Development: A Long-run Comparative View*, Vol. 2, Oxford: Oxford University Press, 1991. Other authors place more stress on the role of international relations, the state-form, class conflicts, technology or capital's internal over-accumulation dynamics. See Robert Albritton, Makoto Itoh, Richard Westra and Alan Zuege, *Phases of Capitalist Development: Booms, Crises, and Globalizations*, Basingstoke and New York: Palgrave, 2001.

Table 3: Bubbles, recessions and golden ages in historical perspective

Wave		Installation period 'gilded age' bubbles	Turning point recessions	Period of deployment 'golden ages'
First 1771	Industrial Revolution (Britain)	Canal mania	1793–1797	Great British leap
Second 1829	Age of steam and railways (Britain)	Railway mania	1848–1850	The Victorian boom
Third 1875	Age of steel and heavy industry (Britain, USA, Germany)	London and Paris funded global market infrastructure build-up	1890–1895	Belle Epoque (Europe) Progressive Era (US)
Fourth 1908	Age of oil, autos and mass production	The Roaring Twenties (autos, real estate, radio, aviation, electricity)	1929–1933 (Europe) 1929–1943 (US)	Postwar golden age
Fifth 1971	ICT revolution (USA)	Emerging markets, dotcom and internet mania, financial casino	2007– ?	Sustainable global knowledge-society 'golden age'?

Source: adapted from Carlota Perez, 'Finance and technical change: a long-term view: research paper', *African Journal of Science, Technology, Innovation and Development*, 3:1 (2011), 10–35.

Consistent with this interpretative framework, Perez sees the contemporary period as an interregnum in which innovations linked to IT constitute the basis for a possible new boom. The realisation of this possibility would require a socio-political reorganisation that remains undetermined.

In their recent bestseller, *The Second Machine Age*, Erik Brynjolfsson and Andrew McAfee very convincingly argue that information technologies have not yet reached the height of their power.[18] They consider that driverless cars, maintenance robots and computerised medical diagnoses will soon become part of everyday life. These innovations, which herald many other technological upheavals, will radically shake up the social conditions for production and could bring immense productivity gains. Yet Brynjolfsson and McAfee forget something essential here – namely, that this is not principally a technological problem but a question of economics and politics. Conversely, one of the strengths of Perez's approach is that she recognises this. For her, technological change is inscribed in a systemic movement that moves at the pace of the profit dynamic. Financialisation is Janus-faced: it is simultaneously both the symptom of problems within the productive sphere and the vehicle of a possible and yet uncertain regeneration of capitalism.

Regarding the socio-economic logics associated with the financial profits examined in Chapter 6, Perez and the upholders of the 'cognitive capitalism' thesis each lay great stress on innovation. The centralisation of capital within globalised and deep financial markets is a powerful tool for reorienting contemporary capitalism toward new fields of accumulation. In this context, financial profits appear firstly as a levy on profits realised in the productive sphere, thanks to the allocation of capital to new sectors of activity or to the modernisation of already established firms. Here, financial exuberance is a collateral effect of an ongoing systemic restructuring. When we leave this factor on the periphery of our analysis, we create a blind spot in our understanding of the relations between finance and knowledge. We already know of the disorienting effects linked to financial exuberance, as pointed

---

18   Erik Brynjolfsson and Andrew McAfee, *The Second Machine Age: Work, Progress, and Prosperity in a Time of Brilliant Technologies*, New York: W.W. Norton & Company, 2014.

out in our discussion of the concept of fictitious capital. In distorting relative prices, financial accumulation leads to a poor appreciation of both risks and opportunities, which results in substandard investment decisions. This is how one Austrian school commentator described the torment of autumn 2008 and the boom that had preceded it:

> All of this new and additional money entering the loan market is fundamentally fictitious capital, in that it does not represent new and additional capital goods in the economic system, but rather a mere transfer of parts of the existing supply of capital goods into different hands, for use in different, less efficient, and often flagrantly wasteful ways. The present housing crisis is perhaps the most glaring example of this in all of history.[19]

The rap battle video 'Fear the Boom and the Bust' sets out this argument rather effectively: when the orgy of credit no longer suffices to prolong the boom, we should watch out for the hangover that follows. Far from producing efficiency, the complexity of financial algorithms, the acceleration of transactions via automated high-frequency trading, and the fragmentation of finance chains have in fact made financial transactions more opaque.[20] As one monetary fund manager candidly admitted at the worst moment of crisis, the apprentice-sorcerers could no longer control their monster: 'the problem is that people just don't know quite what to trust, or not … Probably everything in most of these portfolios [behind commercial paper] is fine, but people don't know for sure, and people don't want to take the risk.'[21] In sum, financial operators did not know what they were doing. This seriously puts in question the quality of the use of available resources that results from such an allocation mechanism. Could it be that, far from favouring investment, financial accumulation in fact impedes it? This question brings us to the problem of the relations between financialisation and the transformations of non-financial firms.

---

19 George Reisman, 'The myth that laissez faire is responsible for our present crisis', mises.org/daily, 23 October 2008.

20 For a mathematically based discussion of the misleading effects of excessive mathematisation see Nicolas Bouleau, 'On excessive mathematization, symptoms, diagnosis and philosophical bases for real world knowledge', *Real World Economics*, 57 (2011), 90–105.

21 Cited in Tett, *Fool's Gold*, p. 177.

CHAPTER EIGHT

The Enigma of Profits Without Accumulation

The works we have just examined tend toward a certain functionalism, presenting finance as the instrument of the metamorphoses of production under capitalism. They portray the immediate instability and harmful social effects as the price that has to be paid for an economic restructuring that will be beneficial in the medium or longer term. We will now turn to examine an opposite interpretation that instead maintains that contemporary financialisation constitutes a barrier to the development of the productive forces. This argument is based on a solid (if stylised) fact: over recent decades, total investment as a proportion of GDP has unevenly but significantly declined in the main wealthy countries (see Figure 23). This deceleration of accumulation is fully consistent with the slowing of growth over this same period.

This dynamic would be no mystery if it were accompanied by a fall in profits; it would be perfectly logical if, in a situation of falling profits, firms had less resources to invest and less incentive to do so. Yet this is not the case. The early 1980s saw the fall in profit rates come to a halt, even if there is a debate over how much of a turnaround this was.[1] Since that point, we have been faced with a phoney capitalism, summed up by the formula 'profits without accumulation'.[2] Figure 24 presents the

---

[1] There is a very rich but rather technical debate on how profit rates are evolving. Nonetheless, upon examining the various relevant measures, we see an unambiguous shift: the profit rate gradually fell from the mid-1960s up to the early 1980s, before then rising again. There is a debate over the significance of this turning point: is it simply a partial recovery, unable to counteract the tendency for the rate of profit to fall, or is it indeed an authentic upturn? For a detailed presentation of the methodological terms of this debate, see in particular Deepankar Basu and Ramaa Vasudevan, 'Technology, distribution and the rate of profit in the US economy: understanding the current crisis', *Cambridge Journal of Economics*, 37:1 (2013), 57–89; Michel Husson, 'La hausse tendancielle du taux de profit', hussonet.free.fr, 2010.

[2] Laurent Cordonnier, 'Le profit sans l'accumulation: la recette du capitalisme gouverné par la finance', *Innovations*, 23:1 (2006), 79; Michel Husson, *Un pur capitalisme*, Paris:

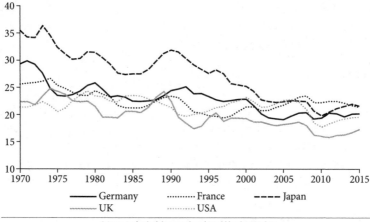

Source: Author's elaboration based World bank WDI data

Figure 23: Gross fixed capital formation (per cent of GDP)

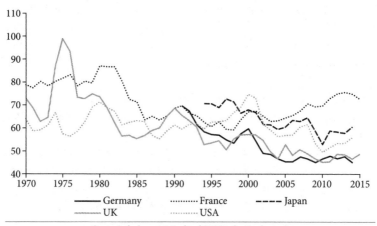

Source: Author's computation based OECD and national accounts

Figure 24: Non-financial corporations' fixed capital
formation (per cent of gross operating surplus)

evolution of the proportion of profits that non-financial firms reinvest.
The retreat is particularly marked in the UK and France, even if in the
latter case the ratio shows something of an improvement at the end of

---

Page deux, 2008; Engelbert Stockhammer, 'Some stylized facts on the finance-dominated accumulation regime', *Competition & Change*, 12:2 (2008), 184–202.

the period in question. In the United States, this movement is lesser in extent and was briefly interrupted in the late 1990s with the new technology bubble. Since the mid-1990s, Japan and Germany have seen a similar loss of dynamism in investment relative to profits.

This configuration is enigmatic from the viewpoints of both classical and Marxist political economy (which assumes profits are reinvested) and the Kaleckian perspective adopted by post-Keynesian economists (capitalists earn what they spend, principally meaning investment).

So how are we to explain this? First of all, we can invoke a phenomenon we examined earlier, namely, the increase in the financial sector's importance within the overall economy. Indeed, this sector, specialised in trading money, has little recourse to investment in fixed capital compared to commercial and industrial activities. But this consideration does not help us clarify the phenomenon described in Figure 24, which concerns only non-financial firms. The phenomenon is often explained in terms of a form of financial parasitism: the demands of the financial markets exert a predatory drain on firms' revenues, driving the latter to reduce investment and push down wages. This is what Laurent Cordonnier and his co-authors maliciously called 'the cost of capital'.[3] Their work portrays 'the rentiers' revenge' as the demands of the financial markets deprive firms of the means to accumulate productive capital and, as a ricochet effect, reduce growth and employment. According to another interpretation, transformations in company governance have driven managers to turn away from the behaviours of the postwar period, reducing their investment in production and privileging financial investments and merger-and-acquisition operations.

As we will see, these two hypotheses are insufficient to explain the phenomenon, because they each omit one fundamental dimension: the knot between globalisation and financialisation, which ties the internationalisation of production processes to the rise of financial payments and revenues among non-financial firms.

---

3   Laurent Cordonnier, Thomas Dallery, Vincent Duwicquet, Jordan Melmiès and Franck Vandevelde, 'Le coût du capital et son surcoût', study by Clersé (Lille 1 & CNRS) for the IRES and the CGT, ires-fr.org, 2013.

THE RENTIERS' REVENGE

The phoney capitalism of the late twentieth century was the result of socio-political struggles in which the property-owning classes emerged victorious. This manifested itself in a rapid increase of the richest layers' share of income and wealth.[4] Up until the mid-1970s, the workers' movement had been on the offensive. Trade unions were powerful and strikes were numerous and often victorious. Yet the productivity slowdown was testament to the exhaustion of the postwar dynamic. Now came stagflation. Growth slowed and profits quickly fell, while high levels of inflation reflected the virulence of the conflict over distribution.[5] In August 1979, Paul Volcker was appointed head of the US Federal Reserve. Under his leadership, the central bank committed to a resolute inflation-busting policy, with spectacular interest rates, peaking at 19.8 per cent in January 1981. Corrected by inflation, up to spring 1982 the economy was subject to real interest rates of some 9 per cent. This decision was anchored in the context of a major ideological shift – a context which Volcker perfectly grasped. In order to make its new policy a success, the FED could 'capitalize psychologically on monetarist support throughout Europe in particular, as well as in the Congress of the United States and much of the journalistic fraternity today'.[6]

In May 1979, Margaret Thatcher came to power in the UK, and the following year Ronald Reagan won the US presidential election. This political turning point allowed for the abandonment of Keynesian policies. Volcker knew that his anti-inflationary policy would provoke a recession, but considering the decline in productivity he thought that there was no possibility of supporting growth. By summer 1982, inflation was sharply declining and he noted with some satisfaction that 'for the first time perhaps in the postwar period, businesses are really looking at themselves. They are not just going through the superficial

---

4   Piketty, *Capital in the Twenty-First Century*.

5   Alain Lipietz, *Crise et inflation, pourquoi?* Économie et socialisme, 36, Paris: Maspero, 1979.

6   Minutes of the Federal Open Market Committee meeting of 6 October 1979. I owe this reference to Marvin Goodfriend and Robert G. King, 'The incredible Volcker disinflation', *Journal of Monetary Economics*, 52:5 (2005), 981–1015.

aspects of counting noses and cleaning house in the conventional ways.'[7] The rise in the cost of credit brought a macroeconomic shock of some consequence. Bankruptcies and rising unemployment brutally undermined workers' power to negotiate. Conversely, the owners of financial capital benefited from the soaring interest rates.

In retrospect, this 1979 coup appears as the founding act of neo-liberalism. Given the central importance of the US economy, its effects spread on a planetary scale. As interest rates rose, rentiers got their revenge. They saw their power consolidated by gradual liberalisation, undoing the tight straitjacket in which financial activities had been tied up since the Great Depression of the 1930s.[8] According to this explanation, the combined effects of interest rate hikes and the liberalisation of finance are at the origins of the investment slowdown. As Figure 25 shows, the rate rise drained companies' own resources. In parallel to this, the profitability of financial operations grew, which led shareholders to demand firms achieve a higher profitability norm. The share of profits that firms held onto thus decreased and investment slowed. Logically enough, proposed investment projects are subject to a harsher selection process, as they must meet this new profitability norm.

To what extent are financial payments acting as a drain on firms' profits? In France and the United States, data are available for a sufficiently long period to seem to corroborate this analysis (see Figure 26a to 26e). In the French case, in the 1970s we can see an increase in the volume of interest paid, accelerating with the rise in interest rates. But in the 1980s, it slowly began to decline as firms lowered their indebtedness. In the second half of the 1990s, there was an explosion of dividends, to the point that the total amount of payments on the financial markets rose from around 40 per cent of gross operating surplus in the early 1970s to over 110 per cent at the moment of the 2008 crisis. Interestingly, buybacks appeared only in the 2000s, and they play a rather limited role also outside of the United States.

---

7   Minutes of the Federal Open Market Committee meeting of 1 July 1982.

8   Duménil and Lévy, *La grande bifurcation*; Jacob Morris, 'The revenge of the rentier, or, the interest crisis in the United States', *Monthly Review*, 33:8 (1982), 28; John Smithin, *Macroeconomic Policy and the Future of Capitalism: The Revenge of the Rentiers and the Threat to Prosperity*, Brookfield, VT: Elgar, 1996.

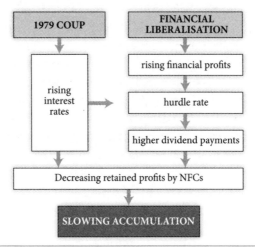

Source: Cédric Durand and Maxime Gueuder, 'The investment-profit nexus in an era of financialisation and globalisation. A profit-centred perspective', Working Papers PKWP1614, Post Keynesian Economics Study Group

Figure 25: The rentiers' revenge and the slowdown of accumulation

In the US, the monetarist shock in 1979 marked the beginning of a rise in the volume of financial payments. Up until the mid-1980s, it was interest payments alone that sustained this movement. The particularity of the US case is the essential role of stock buybacks, which for tax reasons partly substitute for dividends as a means of remunerating shareholders: by repurchasing their own shares, firms push up prices, which mechanically generates capital gains for the owners of these equities. Over this whole period, there was also a major rise in total payments on the financial markets, from an average (mean) of 40 per cent in the 1970s to a landing of around 60 per cent from the mid-1980s onward. Nonetheless, this was substantially lower than the level they reached in France in the 2000s.[9]

---

9   It is not easy to explain the extremely high level of financial incomes and payments that non-financial firms have reached in France as compared to other countries. A first explanation is related to the tax system, which – through social security contributions – heavily taxes firms before profits are declared. Moreover, the variety of consolidation accounting techniques across different national contexts may also contribute to this divergence. Whatever the case may be, this is a qualification in terms of extent, not of the tendencies themselves.

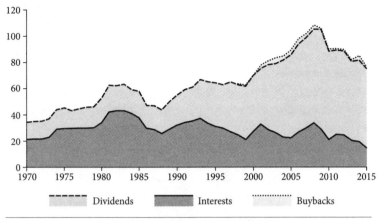

Source: Author's computations based on OECD and ECB data

Figure 26a: Non-financial corporations financial payments –
France (per cent of gross operating surplus)

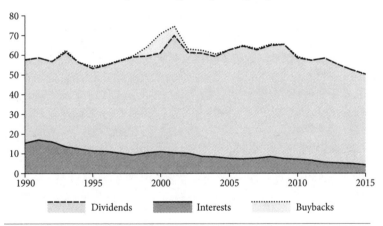

Source: Author's computations based on OECD and ECB data

Figure 26b: Non-financial corporations financial payments –
Germany (per cent of gross operating surplus)

Taking less of a step back in time, we can see that, in the UK, dividends increased in the late 1990s and then stabilised. Germany would see the same type of trajectory a decade later, with increasing dividends more than compensating for declining interest payments in the period before the financial crisis. The notable thing in Japan is the big drop

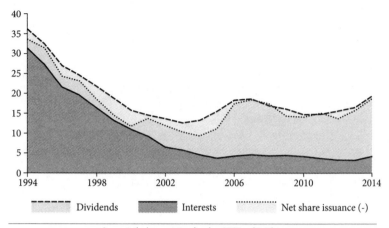

Source: Author's computations based on OECD and BoJ data

Figure 26c: Non-financial corporations financial payments –
Japan (per cent of gross operating surplus)

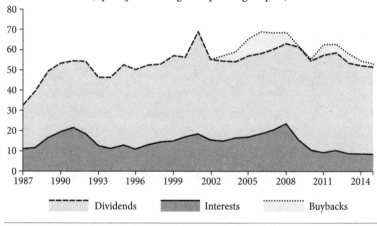

Source: Author's computations based on OECD, ONS and BoE data

Figure 26d: Non-financial corporations financial payments –
UK (per cent of gross operating surplus)

in the interest payments associated with firms' long spell of indebtedness in the wake of the 1980s bubble, yet also the mounting weight of dividends in the 2000s. Financial payments are, however, much less sizeable here than in other countries. It is also worth noting that this is the only country where overall financial payments did not decline as a share of profits in the aftermath of the great financial crash of 2008.

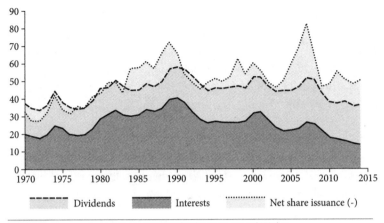

Source: Author's computations based on OECD, BEA and FED data

Figure 26e: Non-financial corporations financial payments –
US (per cent of gross operating surplus)

Where it has taken place, the rise in the share of profits dedicated to payments on the financial markets could suggest that the paradox of profits without accumulation should indeed be explained in terms of the rentiers getting their revenge. Yet, in fact, this thesis is not very convincing. As we will show below, firms have also drawn increasing revenues from their financial activities, to the extent that the resources they have available to invest – as a proportion of their profits – have not noticeably diminished. The financialisation of non-financial firms' revenues thus appears as one of the responses to the transformations of company governance implemented in the 1970s and the resulting aversion toward productive investment.

An aversion to investing

In one oft-cited article, William Lazonick and Mary O'Sullivan describe the maximisation of shareholder profits as a company governance ideology that developed in the 1980s and 1990s.[10] This ideology accompanied a major swing in strategic orientation on the part of big firms' executives. They abandoned the logic of the Fordist period –

---

10   William Lazonick and Mary O'Sullivan, 'Maximizing shareholder value: a new ideology for corporate governance', *Economy and Society*, 29:1 (2000), 13–35.

which consisted of 'conserving and reinvesting' profits in order to max-
imise their firm's growth – and instead aligned with shareholders' goal
of short-term returns. This implied 'restructuring and distributing':
that is, reducing employment by detaching themselves from the least
profitable activities, outsourcing the other roles supporting its main
activity (typically meaning cleaning, company catering, security, maintenance), and developing their use of international sub-contracting in
order to increase the share of profits distributed to shareholders. This
reorganisation was in part a response to the profitability crisis of the
1970s and was inscribed in a context of interest rate rises.[11] But it played
out above all at the microeconomic level. It was a matter of changing
the enterprise itself.

Company restructuring

Up until the 1970s, big, diversified conglomerates predominated. In
the US, most of the leading enterprises in each sector maintained a
dominant position and were also victorious at the international level:
General Motors, Standard Oil, Goodyear, DuPont, Procter and Gamble,
United Fruit and R.J. Reynolds featured among the seventy firms who
counted among the top 100 US companies in both 1919 and 1969.[12]
Such strong stability in the big firms is characteristic of monopoly
capitalism. However, the 1980s and 1990s saw a major reconfiguration
process. Out of the fifty-four US firms who featured among the world's
leading 100 firms in 1912, only seventeen still appeared on this list in
1995, and only twenty-six had a greater capitalisation in 1995 than in
1912.[13] This decline did not result mainly from the rise of the digital
economy's new giants (Microsoft and Apple were at this point still
far from these heights, and Google and Facebook did not yet exist).
Rather, it owed more to a phenomenon linked to a progressive loss

---

11   Neil Fligstein and Taekjin Shin, 'Shareholder value and the transformation of the
US economy, 1984–2001', *Sociological Forum*, 22:4 (2007), 402.

12   Richard C. Edwards, 'Stages in corporate stability and the risks of corporate failure',
The Journal of Economic History, 35:2 (1975), 428–57.

13   Noami R. Lamoreaux, Daniel M.G. Raff and Peter Temin, *Beyond Markets and
Hierarchies: Toward a New Synthesis of American Business History*, National Bureau of Economic Research, 2002.

of the advantages of integration as well as a tendency toward special-isation. The continual reduction of transport and communication costs improved market fluidity and the robustness of transactions. It thus diminished the problems of technical and commercial interde-pendence associated with specific assets, which had hitherto justified vertical integration. Moreover, with rising living standards, demand itself evolved, turning away from standardised products and toward differentiated goods and services. The advantages linked to economies of scale can prove less decisively important in the latter scenario.

Nonetheless, this reconfiguration of the productive fabric did not principally aim at increasing economic efficiency. Rather, it was a matter of shaking up the power relations between shareholders, man-agers and employees. The fall in profits weighed all the heavier on company management on account of the new actors who now counted among their shareholders. In the United States, institutional inves-tors took on an increasing role in the 1970s with the relaxing of the constraints that limited the proportion of risky shares and assets as part of life insurance companies' and pension funds' portfolios. At the same time, collective savings funds developed, and new stock-market techniques and rules allowed the volume of exchanges to be increased and made more fluid. As a result, managers were now confronted with powerful, mobile shareholders very much determined to assert their interests. In the 1980s, shareholder assemblies transformed into a battlefield, and there was a proliferation of hostile takeovers casting aside management teams.

These activist shareholders could lean on a freshly elaborated theoretical apparatus, the 'theory of agency',[14] according to which managers tend to carry out policies guided by the objectives of growth and maintaining employment. These goals correspond more to their own interests than to their shareholders'. Yet restoring the power of the principal (shareholders) over the agent (managers) required a credi-ble threat. It thus suited them to create a takeover market that would allow them to cast aside any company management that did not extract

---

14   Michael C. Jensen and William H. Meckling, 'Theory of the firm: managerial behavior, agency costs and ownership structure', *Journal of Financial Economics*, 3:4 (1976), 305–60.

enough dividends and capital gains on the stock markets. As Jensen concisely put it, 'the problem is how to motivate managers to disgorge the cash'.[15]

Proliferating initially in the United States in the 1980s, Leverage Buy-Outs (LBOs) represent a radical means of achieving this objective. The raider seeking to buy up stock emits debt of mediocre quality – and thus at high rates – whose counterpart is assets in the targeted company. The managers of the preyed-upon company must do everything they can to release sufficient revenue to repay the debt, upon pain of bankruptcy. This forces them to carry out mass layoffs and liquidate assets. For the raider, conversely, the gains are considerable and almost guaranteed. In parallel to this, the spectre of hostile public takeover bids imposes discipline on senior executives.

In Oliver Stone's 1987 film *Wall Street*, Michael Douglas plays the unscrupulous trader Gordon Gekko. In one memorable scene where a shareholders' meeting ousts the company's management, Gekko expounds the credo of the era:

> Greed – for lack of a better word – is good. Greed is right. Greed works. Greed clarifies, cuts through, and captures the essence of the evolutionary spirit. Greed, in all of its forms – greed for life, for money, for love, knowledge – has marked the upward surge of mankind. And greed – you mark my words – will not only save Teldar Paper, but that other malfunctioning corporation called the USA.

The other side of this eulogy to greed is company restructuring. These operations first and foremost concern the most unionised businesses.[16] In so far as wages are higher and social benefits are more generous, there is more value to transfer from labour to capital. This unleashes a cumulative process. In less than a decade, unionisation levels in the United States collapsed, from 25 per cent in 1979 to 15 per cent in

---

15   Michael C. Jensen, 'Agency costs of free cash flow, corporate finance, and takeovers', *The American Economic Review*, 76:2 (1986), 323–9 (p. 323).

16   William J. Baumol, *Downsizing in America: Reality, Causes, and Consequences*, New York: Russell Sage, 2003, p. 133; Kim Moody, *US Labor in Trouble and Transition: The Failure of Reform from Above, the Promise of Revival from Below*, London and New York: Verso, 2007.

1988.[17] This weakened workers' overall bargaining power, to the benefit of capital and top management. Conversely, the will to align managers' and shareholders' interests has translated into spiralling remuneration at the top of the hierarchy. This dynamic toward increasing wage inequality in the first instance concerns company-board and finance jobs. These are the very same personnel whose objective is to conceive the management tools consistent with the principle of creating value for shareholders.[18]

The aporia of creating value for shareholders

The literature devoted to the creation of value for shareholders has worked to provide a theoretical demonstration of this principle and the institutional arrangements that flow from it – not only as concerns shareholders but also for economic efficiency in general. Works on company governance have established a merely self-referential principle that the firm must be run in the interest of its owners.[19] But they have failed to prove that allocating the right to control an enterprise to those who provide it with their own funds is the incentive mechanism that allows for optimal resource use.[20] As we shall see, there are two main reasons for this.

Firstly, the financial markets have become deeper and more liquid since the 1980s. One consequence of this is the establishment of a minimum profitability norm, whose counterpart is the transfer of risk to other stakeholders.[21] Indeed, if shareholders are able to demand and

---

17 Lawrence Mishel, Jared Bernstein and Heather Boushey, *The State of Working America, 2002/2003*, Ithaca, NY: Cornell University Press, 2003.

18 Godechot, 'Financialization is marketization!', *MaxPo Discussion Paper* 15/3, Paris: MaxPo, 2015; Donald Tomaskovic-Devey and Ken-Hou Lin, 'Income dynamics, economic rents, and the financialization of the US economy', *American Sociological Review*, 76:4 (2011), 538–59.

19 This question of firm ownership is not as self-evident as it may seem. Jurists have shown that, from a legal point of view, the firm does not belong either to shareholders or other stakeholders. The crucial question is who governs the firm. See Virgile Chassagnon and Xavier Hollandts, 'Who are the owners of the firm: shareholders, employees or no one?', *Journal of Institutional Economics*, 10:1 (2014), 47–69.

20 Antoine Rebérioux, 'Les fondements microéconomiques de la valeur actionnariale', *Revue économique*, 56:1 (2005), 51–75.

21 Frédéric Lordon, 'La création de valeur comme rhétorique et comme pratique.

secure guaranteed returns, they will not take on the risks of entrepreneurship, which they will instead leave up to others to bear. As we know, the 'others' in question are workers, made to bear these risks through the individualisation of remuneration and an increase in labour flexibility. But they also include suppliers. In our research on big retailers, Céline Baud and I have provided a spectacular illustration of this phenomenon.[22] Over the last two decades, ICT and improved transport have considerably increased the efficiency of the logistics chain. For the ten biggest global companies in this sector, this has translated into an average (mean) one-third fall in the cost of their stock, from forty-nine to thirty-four days' worth of sales between 1992 and 2007 (see Figure 27). Nonetheless, this saving has not reduced the time it takes them to pay their suppliers, even though the latter have also invested in the logistical chain. We can even say that the opposite is the case. In 2007, the ten main distributors' average (mean) debt to other stakeholders (mainly suppliers) represented forty-three days' worth of sales, as against around thirty at the beginning of the 1990s. Such is the extent of this development that the capital advanced by suppliers now not only covers the cost of stocks but even substantially exceeds it.

Suppliers provide their own funds to retailers for free and thus boost profitability and the value distributed to shareholders. A hierarchy of capitals is established in which the centre, directly connected to the financial markets, avails itself of a market power allowing it to transmit conjunctural shocks to the firms situated on its periphery and to push up value in order to meet and exceed the returns guaranteed to shareholders. The pressure transmitted through this chain translates into an erosion of wage conditions in sub-contracting firms, which is ever more accentuated the more distant we get from the order-givers.[23]

Généalogie et sociologie de la valeur actionnariale', *L'Année de la régulation*, 4 (2000), 117–67 (pp. 137, 138).

22   Céline Baud and Cédric Durand, 'Financialization, globalization and the making of profits by leading retailers', *Socio-Economic Review*, 10:2 (2012), 241–66.

23   For an empirical study in this regard based on French data, see Corinne Perraudin, Héloïse Petit, Nadine Thèvenot, Bruno Tinel and Julie Valentin, 'Inter-firm dependency and employment inequalities: theoretical hypotheses and empirical tests on French subcontracting relationships', *Review of Radical Political Economics*, 46:2 (2013), 199–220.

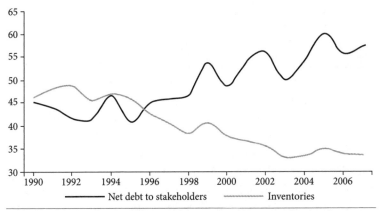

Source: Céline Baud and Cédric Durand, 'Financialization, globalization and the making of profits by leading retailers', Socioeconomic Review, 10:2 (2012) 241–266

Figure 27: Net debt to stakeholders and inventories as number of days of sales among major retailers

The neo-institutionalist approach to transaction costs provides a second argument justifying the assertion of shareholders' disciplining power.[24] In this view, those investing in firms will be exposed to risk, because the funds they bring to the table are invested in specific assets without much liquidity – that is, ones that are difficult to valorise outside the firm itself. But what about the workers? Their involvement in the company by way of the labour process also implies a specific investment – the investment of their own competences, the corollary of which is the risk of devalorisation if they lose their jobs. The same goes for suppliers, who often make considerable investments in order to maintain their position as sub-contractors. Yet we have no reason to establish *a priori* that this risk is any lesser than the risk resulting from managers' use of the funds shareholders bring to the table. This is all the more true given that shareholders have the possibility of freeing themselves from this involvement by way of the financial markets.

24   Oliver E. Williamson, *The Economic Institutions of Capitalism: Firms, Markets, Relational Contracting*, London: Collier Macmillan, 1985; 'Corporate finance and corporate governance', *The Journal of Finance*, 43:3 (1988), 567–91.

Ultimately, the near-guaranteed returns shareholders enjoy in the context of deep and liquid financial markets – as compared to the specific investment made by workers and sub-contractors – imply that they are no more exposed to risks *a priori* than other stakeholders are. Quite the contrary. So there is no basis for considering shareholders better incentivised to control the way in which managers deploy the resources available to the firm. The idea that the strengthening of their power should increase efficiency is thus wholly unfounded.

This inherent theoretical inconsistency is not the only or even the main limitation of the principle of creating value for shareholders. Its assumptions undermine the structure's very foundations. Indeed, in the new theories of the enterprise on which the notion of shareholder value relies, the firm is conceived as a web of contracts among equals.[25] Yet, even when the capital-labour relation is formalised, it relies on a fundamentally unequal contract. This inequality corresponds not only to its dispositions implying the subordination of labour to capital but also to the prior conditions that underlie it. On this essential point, forcefully reasserted by US radicals,[26] it is worth quoting Marx on the relation between capitalist and worker:

> two very different kinds of commodity-possessors must come face to face and into contact; on the one hand, the owners of money, means of production, means of subsistence, who are eager to increase the sum of values they possess, by buying other people's labour power; on the other hand, free labourers, the sellers of their own labour power, and therefore the sellers of labour. Free labourers, in the double sense that neither they themselves form part and parcel of the means of production, as in the case of slaves, bondsmen, &c., nor do the means of production belong to them, as in the case of peasant-proprietors; they are, therefore, free from, unencumbered by, any means of production of their own. With this polarization of the market for commodities, the fundamental conditions of capitalist production are given.[27]

---

25   Benjamin Coriat and Olivier Weinstein, *Les nouvelles théories de l'entreprise*, Paris: Librairie générale française, 1995.

26   Stephen A. Marglin, 'What do bosses do? The origins and functions of hierarchy in capitalist production', *Review of Radical Political Economics*, 6:2 (1974) 1160–112.

27   Marx, *Capital*, Vol. I, p. 785.

Certainly, subordination in the labour process and the dispossession of the products of labour do result from a transaction. But this is a forced transaction. The worker only consents to it because she lacks the conditions to produce for herself and to reproduce her own labour power. Whatever its forms, the wage relation expresses this asymmetry between labour and capital, nestled in capitalism's very foundations: the double separation of the workers from the means of production and the products of their labour.[28] Transformations of the wage relation reflect the need to mobilise labour's creative powers as well as the ways in which power relations develop. But they cannot overcome the antagonism of labour and capital, which is inextricably bound up with the conflict over distribution and political conflict. This is the corollary of a relation of exploitation. This is the primary reason why contemporary political economy gives no credence to the concept of maximising shareholder value. Set in historical perspective, the success this concept has achieved represents nothing more than a capitalist offensive.

Non-financial firms' financial revenues

For the purposes of explaining the enigma of profits without accumulation, it is essential to consider the ideological and institutional offensive associated with the principle of creating shareholder value. Industrial restructuring and the dismantling of sites of strong unionisation have contributed to restoring profits without it being necessary to revitalise investment. However important it may be, this shift does not account for all the effects that the new forms of company governance have on managerial strategies. We must also add a third predicate to the formula 'restructure and distribute': *financialisation*. Managers' alignment of their own behaviour with activist shareholders' demands has indeed led them toward the new sources of profit opened up by the liberalisation of finance and higher rates. Indeed, financial positions offer the advantage of bigger returns without having to make irreversible investments like those corresponding to

---

28   Charles Bettelheim, *Calcul économique et formes de propriété*, Paris: Maspero, 1976.

Source: Author's elaboration

Figure 28: The financial turn of investment and the slowdown of accumulation

investment in production. Figure 28 illustrates the mechanism at work here. Seeking to satisfy shareholders' demands for high short-term returns, company management develops an aversion to irrecoverable costs and diverts part of their resources so that they can valorise them on financial markets. This ultimately translates into an accumulation slowdown.

Figure 29 synthesises the data on non-financial firms' financial revenues presented at the beginning of Chapter 5. The data show a spectacular increase in the financial revenues of France's non-financial firms, thus indicating a turn away from investment in production in favour of financial accumulation.[29] Other countries display the same tendency, albeit to a less marked extent. In the US, it is sustained by capital gains linked to stock buybacks. In all countries except Japan and the UK, we can observe a significant retreat in the weight of this kind of income in the aftermath of the crisis.

The increased importance of financial revenues also shows that we cannot examine the drain on the non-financial sector independently of a consideration of the resources generated by financial operations.

---

29   Mickaël Clévenot, Yann Guy and Jacques Mazier, 'Investment and the rate of profit in a financial context: the French case', *International Review of Applied Economics*, 24:6 (2010), 693–714. We should keep in mind the specificities of the French social contributions system, mentioned above, which tend to underestimate profits as compared to other countries.

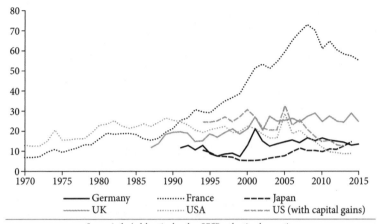

Source: Author's elaboration based on OECD and national accounting

Figure 29: Non-financial corporations' total financial
income (per cent of gross operating surplus)

Figure 30 tracks the evolution of net financial payments as a percentage of the profits realised by non-financial firms. It indicates that there has been no general accentuation of net financial debits compared to non-financial firms' profits. In the US case, we can see a slight progression in the mid-1980s without a clear trend afterwards. Note the spectacular peak in 2007, when companies were heavily buying their own stocks. In France since the 1980s, and in the UK, Germany and Japan since the 1990s, there has been more of a tendency for the weight of net financial payments to fall, with a particularly heavy drop in the Japanese case. This is a very important finding: contrary to what is generally argued,[30] with the possible exception of the United States the financial sector makes no net drain on the resources of non-financial firms.

---

30   For example in Cordonnier et al., 'Le coût du capital et son surcoût'. Attempting to demonstrate the rise in financial debits since the 1990s, the authors of this study resort to a rather dubious methodological patch-up job. They try to correct their ratio between financial payments and investments for inflationary effects. Yet it is hard to understand why, since each of the two terms of this ratio are considered in terms of current prices. This makes their exposition enormously more complicated and leads them to make some truly heroic assumptions (for example, hypothesising the stability of indebtedness levels across the whole period). Moreover, in this operation they omit to subtract the interest that firms receive (pp. 106, 108).

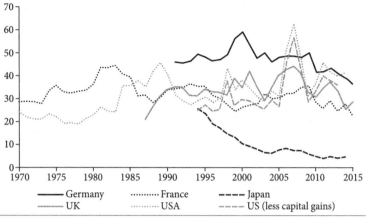

Source: Author's elaboration based on OECD and national accounting

Figure 30: Non-financial corporations' net financial
payments (per cent of gross operating surplus)

Characteristic of today's phoney capitalism is firms' lesser propensity to invest their profits. This tendency is inscribed in an overall
context where non-financial firms have simultaneously both increased
their payments to the financial markets in the form of interest, dividends and stock buybacks, and increased their own financial revenues.
There is no straightforward link between these two dynamics. What
is clear is that the idea that the financial sector is increasingly a mere
drain on firms is a rather unsatisfactory one. After all, the proportion
of net payments to the financial markets is not rising.

We can grasp one mechanism at work here. The increased profitability of financial investments and the strengthening of shareholder
power have negatively affected investment, opening up a new field for
profitable operations and establishing a norm of minimal profitability
beneath which production projects are ruled out. We thus clear up
part of the enigma of profits without accumulation. Financial profits
support non-financial firms' capacity to distribute a larger share of
their profits in the form of financial payments.

Yet this is not a fully satisfactory explanation. While it indicates
that firms have found new sources of revenue outside of the sphere of

production, it leaves the question of the origin of financial revenues largely in suspense. Indeed, taken as a whole, finance does nothing but take from non-financial firms with one hand what it has given them with the other. According to this schema, the financialisation of non-financial firms must be explained in terms of the financial sphere alone. To put that another way: it necessarily corresponds to the dynamic of fictitious capital and the profits-through-dispossession we examined earlier on.

However, there is also another element that needs taking into consideration, for the restructuring demanded by the reassertion of shareholder power has contributed to re-establishing profits without necessitating any new mass investment. Yet here, too, the argument is theoretically insufficient. After all, once the conditions for profitability have been re-established, the share of profits that are reinvested ought to have taken off again on an upward curve.

The shareholders' short-termism remains. And indeed, there is an abundant literature showing how institutional investors, who are forced to report their results very frequently, have transmitted this need to firms themselves. Nonetheless, this explanation is also a problematic one. Share prices reflect beliefs in anticipated profit flows. Accordingly, investment ought to increase anticipated profits, while the profits corresponding to unpaid dividends should translate into a rise in share prices and thus potential financial profits in the form of capital gains. In sum, given that investment also means enriching shareholders, it is difficult to explain managers' aversion to investment as a matter of their obligation to indulge the people who own property in the firm.

If we want to better understand the enigma of profits without accumulation, we ought to turn to factors other than revenues from financial deals alone, and indeed the idea that finance is simply predatory on the productive sector. We will then see that the knot between financialisation and globalisation is a decisively important aspect of this problem.

THE KNOT BETWEEN FINANCIALISATION AND GLOBALISATION

In 1902, the British economist John Atkinson Hobson described what he thought could be the possible end result of imperialism:

> far from forwarding the cause of world-civilisation [an alliance of the Great Powers] might introduce the gigantic peril of a Western parasitism, a group of advanced industrial nations, whose upper classes drew vast tribute from Asia and Africa, with which they supported great tame masses of retainers, no longer engaged in the staple industries of agriculture and manufacture, but kept in the performance of personal or minor industrial services under the control of a new financial aristocracy.

Hobson continued with an exhortation to those sceptical of his claims:

> [Let them] reflect upon the vast extension of such a system which might be rendered feasible by the subjection of China to the economic control of similar groups of financiers, investors, and political and business officials, draining the greatest potential reservoir of profit the world has ever known, in order to consume it in Europe.[31]

For a long time, such a perspective may have seemed absurd. Indeed, the postwar period saw the strengthening of a powerful working class in the rich countries, during a process in which production developed spectacularly. From the 1950s to the 1970s, structuralist and dependency-theory approaches tried to demonstrate that, over time, world capitalism was reproducing a polarisation between centre and periphery. They did this above all with the goal of emphasising the obstacles to development in the poorest countries. Conversely, the 1980s saw acclaim for Japan, Korea, China and Taiwan's success at 'catching up', which was seen as proof that it was possible for such countries to make room for themselves among the ranks of industrialised nations. However, the disaggregation of the Soviet bloc and,

---

31   Hobson, cited by V.I. Lenin, *Imperialism: The Highest Stage of Capitalism*, in *Selected Works*, Vol. 5, New York: International Publishers, 1943, p. 95.

above all, China's insertion into the circuits of world capitalism radically changed the scale of the stakes of globalisation. In this context, Hobson's intuitions seem strangely prophetic.

The world Hobson describes is characterised by three elements: 1) 'a financial oligarchy' dominates the rich countries; 2) the workers of these countries are employed in 'personal services' or 'minor industrial services'; 3) the centre draws a 'tribute' from the peripheral countries in the form of both profits and industrial and agricultural products. We can translate this system of relations into contemporary terms: the financial profits that feed the upward concentration of income in the rich countries are founded on the exploitation of industrial labour and natural resources in the countries of the global South. Industrial activities that have become redundant in the countries of the centre are reduced to their bare bones, with the result that workers in such areas find themselves limited to support or service activities with little added value (personal services in particular), which cannot be traded at the level of international commerce.

Of course, it is not possible directly to transplant such an interpretation onto our own epoch. For example, deindustrialisation cannot be reduced to a transfer of industrial labour from North to South, for it first and foremost results from a well-identified economic dynamic known as Baumol's Law. In a 1965 study on the economic difficulties of New York's performing arts sector, William Baumol and his colleague William Bowen demonstrated that activities in which productivity is more dynamic systematically tend to become less important to the economy and employment relative to those activities in which productivity is stagnant. Thus, between 1913 and today, the proportion of the French population working in agriculture has fallen from 40 per cent to 3.5 per cent, even though production has substantially increased. Conversely, the number of people needed to produce an opera certainly has not diminished, any more than the cost. Any attempt to improve the quality of a performance – in a context where it is not possible to substitute machines for labour – will have to increase the quantity of labour mobilised and thus face higher prices. Sectors like healthcare, education or hairdressing have not seen substantial productivity gains, because the production and consumption of these services demands direct face-to-face contact between producer and consumer. Yet these barriers are not entirely fixed. The development of online university courses and long-distance medical consultations indicates other possibilities for redeploying labour en masse. In May 2012, in a hairdresser's shop in Nishinomiya, southern Japan, Panasonic even tested a robot specialised in shampooing!

The GDP 'catch-up' resulting from capitalist development in the global South in recent years also seems to contradict the classic theorisation of imperialism. Indeed, it is difficult to reduce China's recent trajectory to a simple matter of tributes to the countries of the centre, even as it is about to become the world's biggest economy and thus acquire Great Power status.

Hobson's prediction is less striking for what it is missing – which would hardly be surprising, at a century's distance – as for what it does masterfully grasp: namely, that financialisation and globalisation are linked to one another by the global redeployment of production processes. Figure 31 offers an articulation of this knot between financialisation and globalisation in the recent period. The liberalisation of capitals and trade flows, post-socialist transformation and the end of the developmentalist experiences have opened the global terrain up to the process of capital valorisation. The main consequence of this has been the doubling of the global workforce:[32] as China, India and the countries of the old Soviet bloc joined the world economy, the number of workers on the global market rose from 1.5 to 3 billion over the 1990s. Such a sudden abundance of labour – even if at first this principally means low-skilled labour, whose availability remains partly latent – has exercised downward pressure on wages in rich countries and at the same time offered new opportunities for capital valorisation. This shock is linked to the question of profits without accumulation in the rich countries in two distinct ways. On the one hand, firms can generate profits thanks to the reduced price of the goods they import; on the other hand, the new territories now opened up to international capital offer investment opportunities providing an alternative to domestic investment.

---

32   Richard Freeman, 'The great doubling: labor in the new global economy', eml. berkeley.edu, August 2005.

Source: Cédric Durand and Maxime Gueuder, 'The investment-profit nexus in an era of financialisation and globalisation. A profit-centred perspective', Working Papers PKWP1614, Post Keynesian Economics Study Group

Figure 31: Globalisation and profits without domestic investment

Works on global commodity chains have provided a very broad investigation of this first mechanism.[33] The profit margins of big firms in the global North have increased thanks to the lowered price of imported products, be they intermediate products or, as in the case of the trade sector, final goods. Indeed, the control they exercise over exclusive technologies and access to the most important markets allows them to demand reduced prices for what they purchase without having to pass on these savings at the point of sale. To understand what is at stake here, we shall take the example of US retail giant Walmart.

Walmart is the paragon example of a global buyer in a globalised economy. The firm is both the world's largest company – with a consolidated revenue of $476bn in 2013 – and the world's largest private employer, with 2.2 million employees. It is also an extremely profitable company: since 2010, the Return on Equity of its own capital has never been less than 20 per cent. Each week, 200 million consumers visit its 10,000 sales points, established in twenty-seven countries. With its fleet of thousands of lorries and tens of thousands of trailers, its

---

33   For an introduction to this literature, see Jennifer Bair, 'Les cadres d'analyse des chaînes globales. Généalogie et discussion', *Revue française de gestion*, 201 (2010), 103-19.

hundreds of distribution centres and own satellite system, it enjoys considerable logistical might. For example, it was able to reopen its stores the day after Hurricane Katrina, even before the federal emergency response agency had been able to deploy its rescue operations. Moreover, Walmart is a major actor in the international economy, importing some 15 per cent of the total consumer goods transported from China to the United States.[34]

Given Walmart's economic power, we can easily understand why the balance of forces is little-favourable to most of its 60,000 suppliers. The retailer keeps them in a permanent state of competition, for it can easily switch its supply networks between different companies or even from one country to another. Thus, in order to maintain this often vitally important market, its suppliers will in turn work to reduce their own costs, particularly by resorting to sub-contractors operating on the margins of the globalised economy. The returns obtained by shareholders are thus manifestly connected to the shameless exploitation of labour at the other end of these chains,[35] in particular in the export processing zones which have proliferated across the global South. In 2006, some 66 million people – most of them young women – worked in these areas, where taxes, regulations, and labour rights are almost non-existent.[36] One such EPZ in the Bangladeshi capital Dhaka was the site of the Rana Plaza tragedy. On 24 April 2013, 1,138 workers – most of them women – lost their lives in the collapse of an eight-storey block housing a number of textile workshops. The labels of brands such as Camaïeu, Walmart, H&M, Mango, Auchan, Carrefour and Benetton lay scattered among the debris. On the eve of the tragedy, inspectors had demanded the evacuation of the building after cracks appeared in the walls, but the textile workshop bosses insisted that work resume. The workers were paid less than one euro per day.

34   Emek Basker and Pham Hoang Van, 'Imports "Я" Us: retail chains as platforms for developing-country imports', *American Economic Review*, 100:2 (2010), 414–18.

35   William Milberg and Deborah Winkler, 'Financialisation and the dynamics of off-shoring in the USA', *Cambridge Journal of Economics*, 34:2 (2010), 275–93; Florence Palpacuer, 'Bringing the social context back in: governance and wealth distribution in global commodity chains', *Economy and Society*, 37:3 (2008), 393–419.

36   William Milberg and Matthew Amengual, 'Economic development and working conditions in export processing zones: A survey of trends', International Labour Office, 2008.

We thus have a concomitance between, on the one hand, oligopolistic control of access to final markets and key technologies and, on the other hand, a plethora of labour supply for producing manufactured products and standardised information services. Studies devoted to global commodity chains show that this has contributed to a polarisation at the planetary scale. In their relation to supply networks exploiting reserves of manpower that have only recently been made available, the dominant firms – most of them established in the countries of the global North – can profit from a form of unequal exchange. The spatial heterogeneity of the forms of competition and of development levels in a context of free commodity circulation allows for the pushing up of profits along the whole length of these chains, up to and including the financial markets themselves. Thus, the enigma of profits without accumulation is partly resolved: since profits come not only from domestic operations but also in part from the control of international production networks, it is no surprise that their dynamic has become disconnected from the dynamic of investment.

This thesis is further supported by the growth in imports from non-oil-producing developing countries to high-income countries, which have continuously and rapidly increased from the late 1980s up to today (Figure 32). This is all the more true given that the strengthening of these imports took place in a context of accelerating world trade, up to the crisis.[37] Given the European countries' smaller size and contiguity, they trade a lot more among themselves than the US or Japan trade with other developed countries. This is the essential explanation of the gap between these two groups of countries. But the overall tendency clearly reflects the new proletarians' growing penetration into the valorisation processes controlled by the firms of the global North.

The relations between financialisation and globalisation are also knotted around a second mechanism, operating by way of foreign direct investment (FDI) by firms in the global North. We have already

---

37   Total share of global trade to GDP passed from about 35 per cent in the late 1970s to a peak of 61.1 per cent in 2008. This ratio has since significantly diminished to 57.9 per cent in 2015, fuelling fresh debate about a possible retreat of globalisation. Total trade is measured as total trade in goods and services (world exports plus world imports) as a percentage of GDP according to the World Bank.

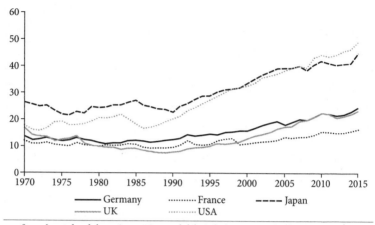

Source: Imports from fuel exporting countries are excluded – Author's computations based on IMF trade statistics

Figure 32: Imports from emerging and developing
countries (per cent of total imports)

mentioned the idea that the small proportion of profits that firms reinvest in their domestic economies is linked to the fact that they also have other opportunities for valorisation. In particular, as we have said, non-financial firms have the possibility of supporting their own profits through financial activities. But globalisation evidently also offers other outlets for capitals from the global North. Over the 1980s and 1990s, the lifting of most of the restrictions on foreign direct investments in the countries of the South gave capital access to gigantic reserves of manpower and natural resources, but also to new markets. This made it possible to substitute foreign investment in developing countries for investment in high-income countries.

Figure 33 bears witness to the dynamism of FDI as compared to domestic investment in the main high-income countries. FDI flows are highly volatile, but the graph speaks to a clear upward trend, at least up until the crisis. While this does not provide a sufficient foundation for the idea that accumulation is being displaced from North to South, this displacement does indeed seem to be taking place. The accumulation slowdown we can observe in the rich countries is not part of a more general movement. On the contrary, Figure 34 shows that, since the 1990s, the size of investment relative to GDP has evolved in the

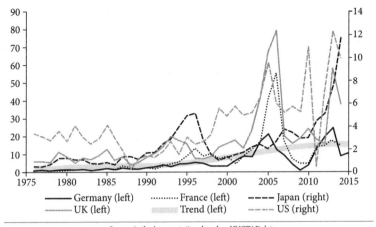

Source: Author's computations based on UNCTAD data

Figure 33: FDI outflows (per cent of gross domestic fixed investment)

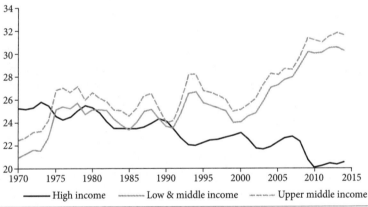

Source: Author's elaboration based on World Bank WDI data

Figure 34: Gross fixed capital formation by group of countries (per cent of GDP)

opposite direction in low- and medium-income countries, in particular on account of the progress of the group of upper-middle-income countries, including China. From 1990, we can even see an inverse and almost perfectly synchronised development of the two groups, suggesting that one is substituting for the other.

This connection between financialisation and globalisation remains little-studied and poorly understood. There are methodological reasons for this. Forty per cent of foreign direct investment flows pass by way of tax havens, and the data on FDI revenues make international comparisons hazardous. In these conditions, it is extremely difficult to give an account of capital circulation processes at a global scale.[38]

One recent piece of research mounted a detailed investigation of data on US firms' FDI. It concluded that the mystery of profits without accumulation is no mystery at all, because non-financial firms are indeed investing, but largely outside of the domestic economy.[39] More particularly, non-financial firms' foreign assets have grown much more rapidly than US and foreign firms' assets within the United States itself. As a counterpart to this, dividends from abroad represent a growing share of all the dividends that firms receive.

New data from the OECD on FDI income allows us to grasp the asymmetry between rich economies and the rest of the world. Figure 35 shows that, for France, Germany, Japan and the US, FDI income far exceeds the payments they make. The margin is minimal for the UK, whose insertion in the global economy is dominated by financial services, for which they receive other kinds of financial-incomes fees from the rest of the world.[40] Of course, these FDI revenues mostly come from other developed countries, but the difference between income and payment is related to uneven FDI-related financial flows between developed and developing countries.

Detailed Banque de France data on the FDI dividends received and paid out break these figures down by geographical area, allowing a further extension of this argument. The data show firstly that, in 2011, the French economy received almost three times more dividends from abroad than it itself paid out. But the offshore financial centres' and the rest of the world's (developing countries') share in the sum of the

---

38   Gabriel Zucman's pioneering works on this theme have begun to lift the veil on the true scale of household assets in tax havens and to question the data suggesting that developed countries are the debtors of developing countries. See Gabriel Zucman, *La richesse cachée des nations: enquête sur les paradis fiscaux*, La République des idées, Paris: Seuil, 2013; 'The missing wealth of nations: are Europe and the US net debtors or net creditors?', *The Quarterly Journal of Economics*, 128:3 (2013), 1321–64.

39   Brett Fiebiger, 'Rethinking the Financialisation of Non-Financial Corporations: A Reappraisal of US Empirical Data', *Review of Political Economy*, 28:3 (2016), 354–379.

40   Brett Cristophers, 'Anaemic geographies of financialisation', *New Political Economy*, 17:3 (2012), 271–91.

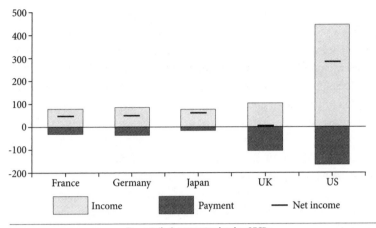

Source: Author's computations based on OECD

Figure 35: FDI income and payments, 2014 (billion US$)

FDI dividends received by the French economy is growing rapidly: between 2005 and 2011, they rose from 2.2 to 8.3 per cent and 12 to 18.2 per cent respectively. While these two groups of countries are sources of dividends, they remain at a stably low level when it comes to the FDI dividends paid from France: almost zero for tax havens and below 3 per cent for developing countries. In short, the investments French firms make in other countries are a large and growing source of their revenues – almost 60 per cent of CAC 40 firms' net returns are realised abroad – and the importance of developing countries is increasing.[41]

Let us summarise: the financialisation of non-financial firms seems partly to be an optical illusion. Certainly, the interest rate hikes of the early 1980s and the acceptance of the ideology of creating value for shareholders contributed to establishing a new profitability norm higher than in the preceding period. Yet this has not meant finance playing more of a predatory role, in the sense of financial payments acting as more of a drain on firms' revenues than they previously did. While financial payments have increased considerably as a proportion of profits, this is also true of financial revenues. Over the long run, this

---

41   D. Nivat, 'Les profits des groupes du CAC 40: quelle contribution des revenus d'investissements directs à l'étranger? Une évaluation sur la période 2005-2011', *Bulletin de la Banque de France*, 192 (2013), 19-30.

has meant that non-financial firms' net financial payments have not increased as a proportion of their profits. In other words, firms seem to pay more financial revenues to their creditors and shareholders thanks to the financial revenues that they themselves generate.

This first reading does not allow us satisfactorily to resolve the enigma of profits without accumulation. There is no doubt that multinational firms have become real financial groups, actively managing their liquid assets in order to profit from opportunities to valorise them at the same time as minimising their outgoings.[42] But the productive dimension of globalisation has also shuffled the pack. For firms in the global North, the liberalisation of trade and investment and the end of the socialist and developmentalist experiences offered new sources of profits and indeed new investment opportunities. These firms could exploit their dominant position in global commodity chains to increase their profit margins as the price of their inputs fell. Moreover, they have rapidly expanded their international operations, including in developing countries, allowing them to meet their shareholders' expectations by way of profits realised abroad.

In sum, the enigma of profits without accumulation is, at least in part, an artificial one. Since the 1990s, the higher profits received by shareholders have increasingly come from the rapid capital accumulation in emerging countries and the profits that this generates. Conversely, firms are turning away from investment in the countries of the global North. This explains their meagre results in terms of growth, employment and wages. Hobson's intuition was correct: the strengthening of the financial oligarchy, the weakening of the workers' movement in the rich countries, and imperialism do indeed make up a system.

---

42   Claude Serfati, 'Transnational corporations as financial groups', *Work, Organization, Labour & Globalization*, 5:1 (2011).

Epilogue

'The market is ... Leviathan in sheep's clothing', the theorist Fredric Jameson tells us; 'its function is not to encourage and perpetuate freedom, but rather to repress it.'[1] Market ideology wears the outward trappings of freedom, but it forbids human beings from collectively and consciously taking their economic fate in hand, claiming that such initiatives can only lead to tragedy. We are lucky to be able to leave things up to the hidden God of the invisible hand, the Smithian market that turns private vices into public virtues and supposedly makes the clash of interests into something harmonious.[2]

This myth leads to an abdication of the freedom to deliberate upon and thereby organise the future. It also means an abandonment of the possibility of revising such plans in tandem with the unfolding of the unexpected. Through the free-marketeer neoliberal project, societies abandon mastery over time to the impersonal mechanisms of finance. The latter thus gains a disciplinary power to which both public and private economic agents have to submit. Bankers' and investors' greed and macroeconomic instability each flow from this mechanism. But what makes up its very heart is fictitious capital: an accumulation of drawing rights on wealth that is yet to be produced, which takes the form of private and public indebtedness, stock-market capitalisation and various financial products.

A decade after the greatest financial crisis the world has ever known, the veil of euphoria has fallen away. Now is the time of disillusionment, where promises no longer work their magic. For almost three decades, financialisation had granted a reprieve to what Wolfgang Streeck has called 'democratic capitalism'.[3] Thanks to rising

---

1   Fredric Jameson, *Postmodernism*, London: Verso, 1991, p. 273.

2   J.-C. Perrot, 'La main invisible et le dieu caché', in *Une histoire intellectuelle de l'économie politique*, Paris: Éditions de l'EHESS, 1992, pp. 333–54.

3   Wolfgang Streeck, 'La crise de 2008 a commencé il y a quarante ans', *Le monde diplomatique*, January 2012; *Buying Time: The Delayed Crisis of Democratic Capitalism*, London and New York: Verso, 2014.

indebtedness and high stock-market prices, firms' profit-needs and populations' aspirations in terms of consumption and public services could each be partly satisfied even despite the sharp economic slowdown as compared to the postwar period. Those who provided credit (shareholders, rich savers, institutional investors) were delighted by the considerable increase in their financial wealth, which they thought was still convertible to money. In some countries, the leading role was delegated to public debt; in others, it was consumer loans and access to home ownership that played the starring role. Some countries – in particular Germany – managed to stem the advance of elementary forms of fictitious capital through their domestic economies by accumulating trade surpluses. Nonetheless, even in this case, the counterpart to some people's surpluses was other people's deficits: and this essentially meant lending to foreigners and accepting financial securities issued abroad. The 2008 hurricane unambiguously showed that nothing escapes fictitious capital's grip.

The crisis came when doubt took hold and the toil underlying the fortunes could no longer keep up with the surge of megabits. As we saw, finance is only relatively autonomous. Certainly, it can tolerate fluctuations operating at some distance from the yields of the real economy. But it cannot free itself from the need to extract profits from land and labour forever. Finance capital may only be a paper tiger, but it bites!

The power that fictitious capital has acquired is embodied in the liquidity of the financial markets. Securities represent a pre-emption on future production, but they also offer their owners the possibility of converting them into real money at any given moment. Collectively speaking, this liquidity is just an illusion, for it would be impossible immediately to liquidate all of these promises. But it is certainly a powerful fiction. Since 2008, the absolute priority that the public authorities have given to financial stability has expressed their determination to validate fictitious capital's claim to liquidity. Yet this claim only holds true if the commitments that have already been made are respected. To put it another way: present financial profits sustain the value of accumulated fictitious capital; the promises made today can only be accepted if past ones have been kept. The great mission of governments and monetary authorities faced with each financial upheaval since the 1980s – and all the more so in recent years – has been to guarantee this continuity of financial profits.

This need today takes on a dramatic and qualitatively novel character in a context of sluggish production. In the rich countries, economic growth has been slowing for almost half a century, and they are now trapped in a secular stagnation. The rise in non-financial firms' financial payments and revenues signals an aversion to domestic investment, feeding these heavy tendencies toward stagnation. And nothing guarantees that accelerated technological sophistication will bring a new phase of economic expansion. As financial promises weigh ever more heavily, our societies are following a trajectory that is both politically and economically explosive.

Fictitious capital's raw material is financial profits. Since finance does not itself produce anything, it must draw its fruits from elsewhere. We have identified three socio-economic logics underlying the accumulation of fictitious capital. If the logic of restructuring production associated with innovation were sufficiently dynamic, then financial profits could be sustained without this inflicting any overly significant damage on society. But the more time passes, the more clearly we see that this is not in fact the case. Financial stability thus comes to depend on two other evidently less worthy mechanisms: dispossession and parasitism.

Dispossession takes the particular form of the political profits associated with the benefits that finance capital takes from state interventions. In the case of aid to the financial sector, these are direct benefits: the public guarantees made to banks as well as unconventional monetary policies coming along in support of equity values. Their social content is opaque: this is, on the one hand, a real or latent charge on the public finances, and, on the other, an enlargement of the monetary power attributed to the financial sector. The indirect benefits are more immediately grasped. The austerity measures running down public services and impinging upon social rights seek to guarantee continuity in the interest payments that administrations pay out. Meanwhile, structural reforms have the goal of supporting firms' profitability – and thus their capacity to pay dividends and interest and generate gains on the stock markets – by reducing the price of labour and opening up new spaces for their operations. Governments' responses to the crisis precisely expressed the logic of dispossession required by a finance sector reigning supreme. For millions of people, this dispossession means catastrophe. It knows no limits other than the political limit to its acceptability; it can only be defeated by social struggle and by the popular masses' capacity to take the initiative. Unfortunately, they have thus far proven insufficient.

The logic of parasitism is based on the maintenance of a minimum profitability level as a financial norm. It serves as a filter on production projects, eliminating even profitable initiatives that do not reach this minimum level. This selection contributes to weakening growth and depressing employment. But it only exists because some of the circuits of capital valorisation offer bigger returns. The forms of unequal exchange between the old capitalist countries and the peripheral economies are crucial in this regard: the insertion of the ex-communist world into the global economy and the abandonment of developmentalist strategies have contributed to feeding the fictitious capital accumulated on the financial markets of the countries of the centre, thanks to the reduced price of imported inputs and to dividends repatriated from abroad. This imperial bonus is the result of a very particular historical conjuncture: three decades during which multinationals have been able to profit from an almost infinite supply of labour, exercise an oligopolistic market power over firms in the global South, and rely on the international predominance of the dollar and – to a lesser extent – the euro.[4] Will the centre's privileges last? Or will the activation of the capitalist dynamic in the periphery inexorably lead to their erosion? These questions go beyond the frame of this book, yet are hardly foreign to its concerns. Indeed, given that the fictitious

4   On the dollar's role in the development of international finance (and, in return, the latter's role in strengthening the pre-eminence of the dollar), see J. Tokunaga and G. Epstein, 'The endogenous finance of global dollar-based financial fragility in the 2000s: a Minskian approach', PERI Working Paper No. 340, 2014. As regards the euro's importance to European banks and multinationals as a global currency project, see Costas Lapavitsas, 'The Eurozone crisis through the prism of world money', in Martin H. Wolfson and Gerald A. Epstein (eds), *The Handbook of the Political Economy of Financial Crises*, Oxford: Oxford University Press, 2013.

capital accumulated in the centre is partly dependent on profits in the periphery, its sustainability also has a geopolitical dimension. In the age of the hegemony of Amsterdam and then London, the competition among international powers was inextricably linked to their financial standing and influence; similarly today, the US's military pre-eminence favours the international role of the dollar and Wall Street's institutions.[5]

In high-income countries, fictitious capital has ceased to be a dynamic factor in accumulation, instead becoming a dead weight on the social reproduction process as a whole. The regulation of financial projections has become chaotic. It proceeds by way of financial and macroeconomic shocks that call for powerful political interventions. The insufficient profits from the molecular process of accumulation-through-production thus make the sovereign state responsible for resolving an ever more acute conflict over distribution, both domestically and abroad. This return of the political is thus paradoxical. The hegemony of finance – the most fetishised form of wealth – is only maintained through the public authorities' unconditional support. Left to itself, fictitious capital would collapse; and yet that would also pull down the whole of our economies in its wake. In truth, finance is a master blackmailer. Financial hegemony dresses up in the liberal trappings of the market, yet captures the old sovereignty of the state all the better to squeeze the social body to feed its own profits. Is this still capitalism? This system's death-agony has been heralded a thousand times. But now it may well have begun – almost as if by accident. Alas, we cannot see any sign of the tomorrows bearing the song of emancipation. Since the plutocrats cannot settle for stagnation, they now resort to a strategy of crushing the rest of us. Capital stole people's hopes. The dead weight of fictitious capital deprives them of what they thought they had won for good.

---

5   Roohi Prem, 'International currencies and endogenous enforcement: an empirical analysis', IMF Working Paper No. 97/29, 1997.

Index